Benjamin Franklin Trueblood

The Federation of the World

Benjamin Franklin Trueblood

The Federation of the World

ISBN/EAN: 9783744728829

Printed in Europe, USA, Canada, Australia, Japan

Cover: Foto ©Suzi / pixelio.de

More available books at **www.hansebooks.com**

THE FEDERATION
OF THE WORLD

BY

BENJAMIN F. TRUEBLOOD, LL. D.

BOSTON AND NEW YORK
HOUGHTON, MIFFLIN AND COMPANY
The Riverside Press, Cambridge
1899

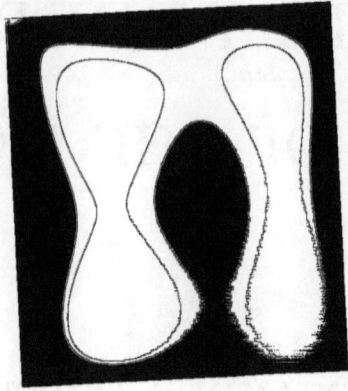

TO

THE FRIENDS OF PEACE

IN

AMERICA AND EUROPE

Pax quærenda pace

PREFACE

HE substance of what is found on
the following pages was originally
given in two lectures delivered before the faculty and students of the Meadville Theological School, Meadville, Pennsylvania, in the spring of 1897, on the Adin
Ballou foundation. The lectures have since
been carefully revised and considerably ex-
panded, and are now given to the public for
the first time. The surpassing interest of
the subject discussed is my only justification
in venturing to bring my thought before a
larger number of hearers than was reached
when the lectures were given. The conclu-
sions reached are the result of many years
of careful study of the international movements of modern society and their causes,
and they cannot be fairly judged except
from the point of view of these movements.

The treatment is original, so far as a great thought, occupying many minds and mouths at the same time, can be treated in an original way by any one person, whose thinking owes so much to that of others. The argument is not intended to be exhaustive, but only suggestive and directive, and it is hoped that it is presented in such a way as to furnish encouragement and inspiration to duty.

The reader will kindly bear in mind that the subject treated is not primarily that of peace and war. These receive a large amount of attention, but only as they are related to the general subject, the federation of the world. The aim of the discussion is to show that the nature of man and of society is such as to indicate that a general federation of the race ought to exist, that war ought to be abolished, that the whole of humanity must move together in harmonious coöperation if it ever fulfills its destiny; to point out the reasons why this federation has been so long delayed; to indicate the influences which have been at work liberating and restoring the federative elements; and to show from actual historic movements and recent social and international achievements that the social and political unity of the world is a consummation rationally to be expected in the not remote future.

B. F. T.

Boston, February, 1899.

CONTENTS

THE FEDERATION OF THE WORLD

INTRODUCTION

WAS Tennyson's dream of " the parliament of man, the federation of the world,"[1] nothing but a poetic fancy, or was it a rational prophecy of an actual condition to be realized in some future, near or far? Is a federation of the world possible? Is it desirable? Is it necessary as an expression of the true nature of the human race, and of its purpose on the earth? If so, what are the signs of its coming? By what means is it to be realized, and in what form? How are the obstacles to its realization to be gotten out of the way?

[1] Tennyson, *Locksley Hall.*

The movements of our time, embracing as they do the whole earth in their compass, are raising these questions in many minds. No more momentous questions, none more startling, none more inspiring, have ever been raised. They involve the widest, the deepest, the most enduring interests of individuals and of nations, singly and combined, in the ages to come. In them are involved also many smaller weighty questions, the solution of which has puzzled, and continues to puzzle, men's brains, — questions of commerce, of finance, of labor and capital, etc., — the solution of which will come about naturally and easily when the larger problems have been disposed of.

The following pages are an attempt to discover what light is thrown upon these questions by the nature of man, the constitution of society, the past and present relations of the nations to one another, and the progress of the federative principle during the century now closing. By way of introduction to the discussion, I may say at the outset that my own mind has reached the clear and settled conviction that a federation of the world is not only possible and easy of attainment, but that it is desirable in the extreme as a fundamental social necessity. A great international state,[1] co-extensive with the surface of the globe, with some sort of government directing the general interests of the race and compatible with local self-government, is the necessary and inevitable outgrowth of the nature of man and of society, under the action of the divinely ordained social processes, and that regeneration and reconstruction of humanity which Christianity is bringing about.

[1] Kant, *Perpetual Peace*, Second Section, 2, near the end. Kant was the first to give us the idea of a great international state. He does not seem, however, to have believed such a state possible. He pleads for a voluntary federation of states as the only realizable means for putting an end to international violence. Of the nature of this federation he gives no clear conception.

The question of the peace of the world, universal and perpetual, is now one of the uppermost in all thoughtful minds. Even those who do not believe that such a state of human society is desirable or realizable are compelled to struggle with the idea.[1] Universal peace, which seemed a little while ago the dream of disordered brains, has suddenly transformed itself into the waking vision of the soberest and clearest of intellects. This world-peace, the signs of whose coming are now many and unmistakable, will not be established between men and nations as so many separate units or groups, standing apart with different and unshared interests, agreeing to let each other alone and to respect each other's rights at a dis-

[1] Von Moltke was accustomed to say: "Permanent peace is a dream, and not even a beautiful dream, and war is a law of God's order in the world, by which the noblest virtues of man, courage and self-denial, loyalty and self-sacrifice, even to the point of death, are developed. Without war the world would deteriorate into materialism." — *Von Moltke as a Correspondent*, translated by Mary Herms.

tance. Such a peace, even if it were possible, would be at best only a negative one,
having little vitality and little power for
good. Universal peace will come rather
through federation and coöperation. The
nature of man remaining as it is, it can
come in no other way. The war-drum will
continue to throb and battle-flags to beat
the wind, armies to be equipped and navies
to be built, until men and nations not only
consider themselves " members one of another," but until they in some large way
treat each other so. All progress in peace
and toward final peace which has been
already made has been made primarily
along this positive line. Abstinence from
smiting with the fist or with the sword is
in large measure the expression in a negative way of a change in men's dispositions
toward each other, which results in positive
mutual beneficence. In this changed disposition the fist spontaneously opens and
the sword falls from the hand. When the
day of universal peace arrives, it will not

find all hatred and disposition to do evil gone, but it will find men and nations so strongly united in the bonds of kindly fellowship and mutual service as to render the disintegrating forces of ill-will practically powerless, — powerless, at any rate, to do mischief on a large scale.

I

The Solidarity of Humanity

EDERATION finds its fundamental reason and its primal necessity in the constitution of humanity. The human race is one race. God "made of one every nation of men to dwell on all the face of the earth." The oneness of origin and descent of the various peoples of the globe is now established with practical certainty on purely scientific grounds.[1] In constitution also is the race one race. The human body, of black or white, of red or yellow, is the same in structure, in purpose and in needs, the world over. The human mind is everywhere built on the same pattern. The highest man and the lowest man can learn each other's language and commune with each other intellectu-

[1] Darwin, *Descent of Man*, Part I., chap. vii.

ally.　Human feelings in all individuals and in all races are the same feelings, however they may vary in degree or manner of expression.　Pleasure and pain, joy and grief, hope and fear, love and hate, are the same affections wherever experienced.　The power of moral determination, though varying widely in its range of activity, is operative in all men, and the capacity for the same moral ideals is likewise everywhere found.　This constitutional unity of the race is practically meaningless on any other theory than that of coöperation and mutual service in working out the destiny of each and all.

The oneness and solidarity of humanity are more strikingly apparent from another point of view.　Men need each other; they cannot live without each other.　Husband and wife, parent and child, brother and sister, live through and for one another.　Beyond the family circle, neighbor needs neighbor, one family another family, one community another community.　The family that eats all its own wheat and corn, its own pork and beans, that weaves its own cloth out of home-grown fibres, that makes its own clothing, tans its own leather, makes its own boots and shoes, shoes its own horses ; that sells nothing and buys nothing from others, that has no minister or teacher outside of its own members, may become a keen and shrewd, nay, even a good little society within its own narrow limits.   Such a family, if it were possible, would, however, lead a meagre and precarious existence, and always remain a narrow and stunted society.   Its members could not rise high in the scale of that intelligence, largeness of spirit, self-control, and altruistic thoughtfulness which constitute men truly human.   So strongly is the need of the companionship and help of others felt, for spiritual as well as for commercial reasons, that families have rarely been willing to live in this isolated way, except under the stress of great necessity, as in pioneer life. Not only in the great migrations of history, but in all sorts of colonial settlements, men have gone together in companies larger or smaller. So great is the enjoyment as well as the practical necessity of association, that most families would rather live near one another and fight than at a distance and be at peace.

Social dependence and the necessity of mutual helpfulness, as fundamental facts of human nature, grow much more marked as the race becomes more numerous and society more complex. A farmer whose family has given up or never learned shoe-making, horseshoeing, weaving, spinning, and the like, because it is more profit-able and agreeable to follow agriculture as a specialty, becomes poverty - stricken and helpless the moment he finds himself unable to deal with the stock-buyers, grain-merchants and grocers. He may com-plain of the village or city as much as he likes, of its dainty-fingered inhabitants and of all the lines of trade which centre there, but you will see him heading that way

every week just the same. The city folk,
too, may look with something like contempt
on the " long whiskers," the " horny hands "
and the workaday clothes of the country
people, but they are always delighted to see
them come in with their loads of grain,
their buckets of butter and their fluttering
coops of ducks and chickens.

Any great city like New York or London, in the advanced state of social development which such a city implies, is always
within a week of starvation [1] if suddenly cut
off from the rest of the world. Every clime
and every industry contributes daily to the
supply of its needs. It raises not a bushel
of wheat, not a load of corn. It fats no
beeves or swine. It produces not a ton of
coal, not a board of lumber. The wool and
cotton which it uses are grown far away

---

[1] Edward Atkinson, speech at the American Conference on International Arbitration, held at Washington,
D. C., April 22 and 23, 1896, says that the world is
always within a year or less of starvation. See Report,
p. 47.

from its borders. When the carts cease to come in from the suburban gardens, the trains of freight to thunder into its stations, or the boats of merchandise to drop anchor in its harbor, it becomes at once as helpless as a child, and begins to cry out for the breast of the great world-mother. A strike on a modern street-car line deranges the plans of every home in a city; a strike on a great railway system throws every corner of the land into confusion.

This interlacing and interdependence of individuals, of families, of communities and of classes, in every relation of life, might be traced out, with interest and profit, *ad libitum.* But the lesson is as clear from the cases given as it could be made by any multiplication of the number. The curious thing about this fact is that men in their normal condition create, spontaneously and intentionally, by the very necessities of their nature, the conditions which, while making them indefinitely stronger and more prosperous when united with their fellow-men, render them more and more helpless when left to themselves.

The dependence of nations on one another is exactly the same in kind, though at first sight not so apparent. The fact that some of them occupy large sections of the earth's surface, and have such a wide range of interdependent activities within their borders, has led some people to the hasty conclusion that they are exceptions to the great law of human interdependence. Only in them, however, does this law have its final, its highest and most efficient fulfillment. Our time is rapidly discovering this to be true, and this discovery is to prove the greatest lever for lifting the world that has ever been dreamed of. Great deeds of unsurpassed beneficence will be wrought when the whole race shall put forth its intellectual, moral and social powers in the freest and fullest combination and harmony. This is a prophecy which is even now writing itself legibly on society without the intervention of a man's hand.

As has often been stated by economists, some nations are so situated in respect of the physical conditions of the earth that they would lead a half-starved existence if compelled to live without intercourse with others. The whole of Great Britain, with her present dense population, would soon grow almost as poor as the poorest sections of Ireland if it were not for her large intercourse with other lands. At the present time this intercourse furnishes the basis of nearly all the occupations by which her citizens live and prosper. Many of the wars of former times had their root-cause, in considerable measure, in this international, inter-racial or inter-tribal need. People were too selfish and narrow to satisfy this need in a normal and friendly way, and hence were driven by their necessities to try to satisfy it in the barbarous and destructive way of war. Much of the friction still existing between the nations results from the pressure of this imperious necessity of international traffic against the selfish and shortsighted nationalism which erects barriers of one kind and another to shut off one section of the earth from natural and healthy intercourse with other sections. The pressure will continue until it has conquered and destroyed the spirit of national exclusiveness ; for however illiberal any people may itself be, no people is willing to be shut out from participating in the advantages which others possess over it. It feels that it has a natural right to a share in whatever blessings any portion of the earth offers, and all nations will insist on this right until they obtain it — and, what is more, till they become large-hearted and sensible enough to *give* it.

In matters pertaining to mind and character also, nations are the complements one of another. France and Germany are not more unlike in soil and climate than they are in the physical and psychical characteristics of their people. This statement is not intended to cover up the fact that these two great peoples, as any other two peoples,

have more similarities than differences. But
the differences between them are so marked
that they greatly need each other, in order
that they may both do the most for their
own material and spiritual development
.and for the civilization of the world. The
estrangement between them, because of the
evil influences of the utterly inhuman system of militarism, is wholly unnatural. They
ought to be, normally, the greatest friends
in Europe. If the money which they spend
and the effort which they put forth in trying to outwit and humiliate each other
were employed by them in doing each other
mutual services, they would be the two central pillars of European civilization. As it
is, their service to humanity is very much
neutralized by their intense mutual anti-
pathy. They are the peril of the whole
Old World, the peril of all the acquisitions
of civilization. A similar charge may be
brought against a number of other nations
in their own spheres. The stupendous iniquity and the far-working mischievousness

of national self-sufficiency are coming to be clearly recognized by an increasing number of people in all countries, to whom the truth has impressively come that nations cannot, any more than individuals, live unto themselves.

All well-read persons are familiar with the thought, often expressed by a certain class of our citizens, that the United States, because of the greatness of her territory, the variety of her soil and climate, the vigor and intelligence of her people, could and should live unto herself ; that she should produce everything which she consumes, and in general get on without the rest of the world. A great variety of excessively righteous and patriotic motives are given in support of this position. This view has just enough superficial reasons in its favor to carry away people of narrow vision and little thought. It is the kind of intellectual pabulum which the hurrah-patriots deal out, highly seasoned, in unstinted quantities to their sentimental followers. But this theory consistently carried out, as the chauvinists, its originators, never do carry it out, would require us to keep at home the eight hundred millions of dollars' worth of products which we annually sell to the rest of the world, call home all our diplomatic and consular representatives abroad, shut out all foreign comers, cease to travel among other peoples, take all our ships off the ocean, write all the books and papers which we read, create our own science, our own art, our own everything. The theory needs only to be stated clearly, to receive immediate and utter condemnation. What these selfish, narrow-minded people really mean is that we should get all we can out of other peoples, and give little or nothing in return, — a position repugnant to every principle of justice and honor, of economic development and prosperity.

It is unquestionably true that the United States could live alone, and live better than any other section of the world could so live. But we could not live thus as we ought to live,—the large, rich, human, useful life that we have been in a measure living, and that we are destined more and more to live, if we keep clear of the sin of hating, irritating, and fighting other peoples. The United States is not the whole world. There are numberless treasures which we do not possess. There are things which we can never grow, or grow only with great waste of energy. There are markets which we cannot duplicate at home, and whole argosies of products which we must sell abroad or let perish in field or storehouse. There are phenomena of earth and sea and sky which no citizen of this country has seen, or can see, without crossing the seas. In brains as well as in climate God has not given us everything. There are thoughts which we cannot think, originally. There are books which we never could have written, discoveries of science which we could not have made, conceptions of high art entirely beyond our intellectual range. We draw

our life from everywhere. We owe our
very existence to the Old World. Europe
is the mother of us all. Our history all
begins on the other side of the sea. Our
life is fed thence in a thousand ways. The
Old World and the New are, commercially,
intellectually, morally and socially, as much
parts of each other as the two halves of
the planet. The same is true of all parts
of the race in reference to one another, as
might be illustrated indefinitely. If there
is any earthly fact perfectly clear to all
sane minds, it is that the human race,
physically, intellectually, morally, socially,
economically, is one race; that it has one
great joint habitation, one broad varied field
for the exercise and unfolding of its capa-
cities; that its interests are one, that it has
a common destiny.

II

Solidarity Unrealized

THIS solidarity of humanity, founded in the constitutional unity of the race, and in that divergence in characteristics which renders all peoples necessary to one another for the highest individual, national and racial development, has as yet been poorly realized. Between many parts of the world there have appeared but the vaguest traces of it. Between great nations, calling themselves civilized and Christian, there is still an appalling lack of it. They have accepted as much of it as the irresistible tide of progress has compelled them to accept. Along a few lines voluntary efforts have been made to realize solidarity in its worldwide aspects, but these have been weakened and much hidden from view by the continuance of the old struggle for individual and national mastery, with its blind disregard for the rights of others and their power of return services.

The sin of the world has been that the race of man, instead of being a loving, co-operating, united race, as it was destined to be, and as it some day will be, has been a hating, fighting, distracted, broken one. The law of life in general has been every man for himself and against every other man as much as necessary for selfish ends. Of the exceptions to this law and of the movements of another law, "struggle for the life of others," [1] something will be said later. Even in the family, where from the beginning of history the sense of dependence, of regard for others, of solidarity, has been most strongly felt, the law of hate and strife has held sway. If the world's history could be fully written, no chapter would be more distressingly interesting than that on family quarrels. It would

[1] Henry Drummond, *The Ascent of Man*, chap. vii.

be copious enough to satisfy the curiosity of the most confirmed gossip-monger. It would be well for the world if its other quarrels had been attended by as much feeling of shame, and they had been as carefully concealed as its family quarrels.

When the first families began to branch off and to develop into tribes, the feeling of oneness and solidarity, which, in spite of strife and contention, had been preserved to a considerable degree by the immediate necessities and affections of the family, began rapidly to disappear. Appetite, passion, greed, the desire for mastery, prevailed over the sense of kinship, right and duty. Within the various tribes, beginning from each particular family, the same process went on, resulting in internal strife and division. A little way down the diverging lines of descent the sense of kinship and fellowship often, in appearance at least, disappeared entirely. Forests, rivers and mountains, once passed, made intercommunication difficult; means of preserving an-

cestral records were few ; language changed
rapidly ; and as the clans and tribes wandered on they often became entirely unknown one to another, and to those left
behind.   In this way, when by any chance
peoples in their wanderings met, or fell in
with other peoples of more fixed habitation, they came to seem to one another of
an entirely different race and origin, or, if
kinship was suspected, the sense of it was
overpowered by the selfish instincts and
determinations.

Neighboring tribes sometimes preserved
some feeling of oneness and mutual interest, especially where their dispositions and
physical surroundings kept them for long
periods in the same region until they developed into a people more or less homo-
geneous, or where they found themselves
compelled to unite in common defense
against aggressors.   But neighboring tribes
more often fell into strife and engaged in
petit wars of conquest and revenge.   Feuds
grew up which lasted generation after gen-

eration.   Strong tribes became aggressors
and enslaved weaker ones.   The leaders of
the conquering tribes became warrior kings,
whose selfish ambition for wide-reaching
conquests often knew no bounds.   Through
them grew up little and great monarchies,
with their bloody exploits, their slaveries
and their tyrannies.

It is impossible to trace this wreckage of
brotherhood, this failure to realize solidarity, as it worked its way down in history as
families became tribes, tribes peoples, and
peoples nations.   When we reach that point
where historic records become clear and
trustworthy, we find men, tribes, peoples,
nations, everywhere hating, fighting, plun-
dering, enslaving and destroying one another.   Not literally at every moment has
this been true, or in every region.   The
work of destruction has often ceased from
sheer exhaustion on one or both sides, until
strength has been recovered for new on-
slaughts.   It must not be forgotten that
family connections and affections have al-

ways tended to restore within certain limits the sense of brotherhood and oneness. So, too, right and duty, love and beneficence, have sometimes asserted their power even between alien peoples. Nevertheless, the one feature of history, standing out above all others, has been the hating, quarreling and mutual destruction practiced by men of all ages and of all climes. This kind of history is still making itself. Within the borders of nations there has been a great change. Here civil order and peace for the most part prevail. Private war, dueling and personal fighting have almost disappeared. By the action of the collective will of the social body law has taken the place of violence. But between the nations hate and violence still have it very much their own way. To what extent a better spirit is prevailing, and may be expected further to prevail, in international affairs, and by what means the change is to be brought about, will be examined later.

III

The Causes of the Disunity

WHAT has been the cause, or causes, of this hideous historic phenomenon? There have been several causes. Lack of moral development is the general cause assigned by the evolutionary philosophy. If this means lack of moral capacity, that men did not and could not know any better, it doubtless played some part in the earlier ages, and in specific cases all the way down. But it is difficult, on any intelligent reading of authentic history, to give this cause the foremost place, or even any considerable place, in the production of the animosities and wars which have prevailed. It is impossible to believe that the wars of this century, or of any other recent century, have been waged by

peoples or rulers who had no moral conception of the iniquity of which they were
guilty and no power to abstain from it.   It
taxes to the utmost one's power of belief
to hold this view of the great contests
recorded in ancient history.   Had Rome
and Greece no conscience and no power of
self-control?   Were Babylonia, Persia, the
Egyptian dynasties and Carthage merely
acting as irresponsible children, in their
wars of conquest and of revenge?   Whatever may be true of prehistoric or of early
historic men, the time went by many centuries ago when wars were nothing more
than the expression of the struggling forces
of beings who had no moral light to guide
them.   The simple fact that they judged
and condemned one another for injustice,
for deeds of the same sort as were done by
themselves, is all the proof of this position
that it is necessary to bring.

Turning this evolutionary reason another
way, the animalism in man is assigned as
the cause of the phenomenon.   Certainly,

exhibitions of greed and passion, and brutal deeds superficially resembling those of savage beasts, have abounded beyond numbering in all human history. But whoever takes the trouble to think the matter through knows that no species of animal has ever been known whose members have quarreled and fought among themselves intentionally, intelligently, systematically, and generation after generation, after the manner of men. The animalism in man, which has furnished in a way the basis for his tyrannies, robberies, animosities and destructive violence, has had connected with it something of which the animal knows nothing, — something which, if used as it might have been used, would have made the records of the past very different from what they have been. The bloody history of the world has been human history, not animal history. It has therefore been in large part, and always in some part, wicked and criminal history. It is a cheap and unworthy method of accounting for the

bloody abominations of our race to assign as
their principal cause an irresponsible and
uncontrollable animalism.   On such a theory there can be no moral criticism of history.   It is not strange, however, that such
a theory is adopted.   All of us at times
blush to be connected with a species of
being the conduct of whose members has
so often been, and still is so often, diamet-
rically opposite to all that might have been
expected of them.   But nothing is gained
for the truth when we wipe out the responsibility of our progenitors, and of many of
our contemporaries, by coolly passing them
through our psychological matrix and transforming them into apes and tigers.   To do
this is no credit either to ourselves or to
the wild beasts.   Whatever the poets may
say, men have never been, in historic times
at least, apes and tigers, except as they
have made themselves such.

Another reason, akin to the foregoing,
which has been assigned for the phenomenon in question, is heredity.   But this has

not been the primal cause. Men began to
fight before heredity had had time to work
in any wide way. They have continued to
fight, in the most atrocious ways, in those
countries where base inheritances are supposed to have been largely mastered by
intellectual and moral training. Men have
gone to battlefields direct from Christian
churches and Christian homes, with generations of Christian blood in their veins,
and have voluntarily joined in committing
deeds about the details of which every soldier with a conscience is always silent.
Heredity, by its transmission of bad instincts and dispositions, has played a serious part in the maintenance of strife and
violence in the earth. But if it were the
chief cause, all our efforts for the banish-
ment of hatred and war would be perfectly
hopeless. Heredity, because it is a con-
trollable factor, is to play just as prominent
a part in the creation and maintenance of
universal and perpetual peace, when men
decide to have it so.

Ignorance also has done much to keep alive the spirit and practice of war. Not ignorance in general; for the most intelligent nations have done most of the hard, destructive fighting; so much so that one is inclined at times grimly to think that the chief evidence of civilization in men is the highly developed disposition and capacity to cut each other's throats scientifically and gracefully, or to blow each other into fragments in the speediest and most wholesale way. The ignorance meant is that which nations show in respect to one another. Some of this, — much of it perhaps, — among the earlier and ruder peoples, whose opportunities of intercommunication were few, was unavoidable and therefore pardonable. But in later times the woeful ignorance which peoples have exhibited in reference to almost everything pertaining to other peoples, except their faults and follies, has been quite as much the effect as the cause of their mutual hatreds. This ignorance, largely voluntary and therefore criminal, has been and still is one of the chief bulwarks of the war system. Hiding behind it, the citizens of one nation conjure up every imaginable ill intent on the part of those of another. Out of the consequent suspicion and fear grow armies and navies and war budgets. This criminal international ignorance is one of the worst foes with which the friends of humanity have to deal, for at its heart is found the real cause of the disunity of humanity.

Another of the potent influences which have coöperated to produce this monstrous phenomenon of history is false education. Fathers have taught their sons to hate those whom they have hated, to keep the fires of vengeance burning on the family hearthstone until offenders against their rights were overtaken and slain or beaten down and enslaved. Aggression and conquest have been taught as a duty. Mothers have sung their children to sleep with ballads of enmity and strife, and entertained them during their waking hours with stories of battles and with toy implements of war, until the imaginations of the little ones were filled with pictures of blood and cruelty, and their young spirits charged with the frenzied desire to rush forth to fight and to slay.   From their earliest years the children of the past, in home and school, have been fed on hostility and war. In this way the larger human affections have been greatly stifled and the voice of conscience often nearly silenced.   When the children have grown older they have, in spite of the protests of their moral nature, voluntarily repeated the error and passed it on.   The leaders and guides of peoples have been deeply guilty of this sin. Statesmen and public orators, priests and ministers of religion, historians and poets, have inculcated a love of country which meant little else than hatred and contempt for other peoples, and eagerness to injure and destroy them on the slightest provocation.

Much is said nowadays about the evil

influence of the detailed descriptions of battles found in school-books of history. This influence is bad enough, certainly, especially when these descriptions are coupled, as they so often are, with the idea, openly asserted or implied, that war is the noblest and most glorious of all callings, that there is no heroism, no manliness, like that of the soldier. But this war teaching of the school-books does not begin to equal in mischievousness the false conceptions of patriotism,[1] the exaggerated notions of the greatness and goodness of one's own country, the disregard and contempt for other lands, which are inculcated not only in the schools, but practically in all the circles of society. The unity of humanity, to any

---

[1] Tolstoy (*War and Peace*, and other writings) holds that patriotism is the cause of most of the existing international evils, and that these evils cannot be destroyed without the abolition of patriotism. If he had used the adjective "false" in connection with patriotism, his position would have been essentially true. A patriotism consistent with Christianity and the notion and practice of universal brotherhood is certainly possible.

great extent, cannot be attained until these false notions of patriotism cease to be held and taught, and the true relation of country to the rest of the world is properly understood and inculcated.

Back of all, running through all, and giving potency to all these causes which have coöperated in different ways to make the world a veritable field of strife and blood, has been the voluntary selfishness of men and of peoples. War, with its multiplied horrors, has not been primarily the outcome of blind forces helplessly contending with one another, but the result of self-directed purposes of beings who turned the light within them into darkness. Evidences abound in history for the truth of this position. There has always been moral perception and moral strength enough in every people with a fairly well developed civil and political organization to have kept it, if it had "minded its light," at least from the sin of aggressive wars, wars for simple vengeance and wars for glory. And these wars constitute the bulk of the war history of the world. Of the moral responsibility of the unorganized, wandering peoples of early historic or prehistoric times it is more difficult to speak. Evidences are coming to light through recent ethnological investigations that even these peoples were not the mere fighting animals that they have been supposed to be. The most primitive peoples now existing, like the Eskimos, have, some of them, no warlike customs.[1]

The guilt of rulers and of peoples for their wars has not of course been equally distributed, for the moral capacity has not been everywhere the same. In many cases single individuals, or a few leading spirits, with commanding powers of influence, have been the guilty cause of a people's or a nation's tyrannies and aggressions, the people following them blindly and slavishly. In truth, this has been the rule in all ages and among nearly all peoples. The bloody annals of the world are, for the most part,

[1] *Encyclopedia Britannica*, article " Eskimo."

records of movements at whose centres
have been powerful and unscrupulous individuals, or small groups of men. You have
only to cast over in your mind the war
history of any nation, as of France, Italy,
Austria, Russia, Spain, or even of Great
Britain, to realize how much of it has been,
not the history of the people, of their life
and purposes and struggles, but the history
of those military tyrants, ambitious princes
and headstrong statesmen who have either
enslaved the people and forced them to do
their will, or blinded them with false hopes
of gain or glory, and so deceived them into
their iniquitous service. The people have
without doubt often shared the guilt of
their leaders, but it is only in recent generations, since the establishment of popular
government, that they have had to bear
the chief burden of guilt in the case of any
particular war. War has been the business
of sovereigns and their minions, not of peoples. Just in proportion as peoples have
become their own rulers, has war begun to
disappear.

At bottom, then, to follow out the thought, war has always been a *sin* of somebody, and not simply a misfortune, not a mere freak of animalism, not a necessary phenomenon of society at a certain stage of development. Whatever other elements may have coöperated in producing it, — ignorance, heredity, false education, — the whole bloody history has been fundamentally a history of sin and wrong. Without the element of iniquitous choice, all the other causes would have operated much less powerfully, or would not have operated at all.

IV

The Development of the War System

OUT of this evil root has come the war system of the nations, which in its elaboration of armaments on land and sea has recently grown to such enormous proportions that it now constitutes the chief burden upon human society, the chief obstacle to its material and spiritual progress. In these great and ever-increasing armaments is found the largest and completest expression of the disunity of humanity. This system must have brief notice before we pass to the consideration of those efforts and influences which are working out the federation of the world and the ultimate abolition of war.

In the far past two boys or men came for some reason to hate each other, and fought

with their fists and feet; or one man in
hunger, greed or envy rose up against another, smote and robbed him, the latter
defending himself or afterwards retaliating.
Something like that, among children or
among men, was the beginning.[1] The whole
war system was there in embryo, in those
two hating, raving, pounding pieces of humanity. Clubs and stones were soon ap-
propriated, in order to add to the offensive
and defensive might of the fist. These
made fighting more complex and more
dangerous. The two men multiplied into
families and clans, which envied, hated
and pillaged each other; which fought, and
fought again. The primitive aggressive-
ness and animosity grew intenser through
acquired dispositions. As the race multiplied, the spirit of contention and strife

[1] The story of Cain and Abel, as given in Genesis,
whatever interpretation may be put upon it, clearly in-
dicates that in the minds of the early historic men fighting had a moral and not merely an animal origin. Cain,
in the record, is under the condemnation of the conscience of his time.

deepened and widened. The stone and the club were supplemented by the sling, the spear, the battle-axe, the bow and arrow, and the sword. Men learned to fight in groups, at first as chance or instinct or interest impelled them. Then, to increase their efficiency, they began to fight under leaders and with some sort of organization and training. War at last became an art on sea and land. More brains and skill went into it; and at the same time more hate and death and woe. War became also a profession. To relieve the rest of the people, that the nation might be always ready for offense or defense, soldiers were trained and kept, whose business it was to fight. Thus grew up standing armies. War became a pastime. When there was no war at home, soldiers let themselves out, or were let out by their sovereigns, to fight for pay or to relieve the monotony of idleness.

As the system developed, watchwords and battle-cries were invented, in order to increase the unity and to strengthen the courage of the combatants. Standards were devised and carried aloft as rallying-points, or symbols of leaders, clan, or country. In order to relieve fighting of its hideousness and to draw attention away from its agonies and groans, uniforms were put on and made resplendent, and martial music was brought into service on the parade ground and on the battlefield. Systems of tactics were thought out — everything, in fact, which intellect, sharpened and perverted by lust and hatred could do, was done, that men might be induced to go out with spirit and daring, with fury and recklessness, with skill and endurance, to beat down and destroy such of their fellow-men as might chance to be called their enemies. Victories were celebrated with noisy rejoicings, with sacrifices to the deities, with *Te Deums* to the God of mercy and love, whom men had turned into a being of hate and favoritism like themselves. Men of daring and bold deeds of blood were honored in song and story, were crowned and lionized beyond all

others. Thus war became in men's eyes
the most glorious of callings, the pathway
to honor and fame, and they blinded themselves to its horrors and its crimes. Pride
and vanity united with lust, greed and
revenge, to clothe the bloody monster in
the trappings of heaven. God became the
god of armies, a regular blood-wading Mars,
appealed to by all combatants to give his
favor to their side. The battlefield grew in
honor as the chief school of the so-called
manly virtues. Women became possessed
of the spirit of war, and nursed their boys
at the breast of aggression and revenge, of
pride and pomp and glory, and took only
soldiers, if they could get them, as husbands
for their daughters.

As the war system [1] developed and made
all peoples its slaves, every discovery of
science, every invention adding to human

[1] Charles Sumner, *The True Grandeur of Nations*
and *The War System of the Commonwealth of Nations.*
Rev. Reuen Thomas, D. D., *The War System, its History, Tendency and Character in the Light of Civilization and Religion.*

power, was immediately turned into an instrument of conquest, of revenge, of destruction and death. Sovereigns and peoples, in this emulation of brute force as the instrument of passion, greed and violence, failing to find sufficient mercenary or voluntary force to outdo their neighbors, resorted to forced levies and conscriptions, and, to meet the ever-growing demands for money, adopted the ruinous and irrational expedient of war loans, and took to mortgaging the future. Business of every kind, home life, civic interests, education, religion even, had to fall down helpless at the feet of the war-god. Differences, small and great, between sovereigns were submitted to the blind and senseless arbitrament of the sword. Might became right, and justice between peoples wandered outcast and homeless. Honor and patriotism — the former merely a euphemism for excessive and irritable self-esteem personal and national, the latter a blind worship of self under the impersonal guise of country — became the criteria of duty.

In all these ways the barbarous war system has grown and grown until it stands to-day, in appalling magnitude, fortified to heaven in the very heart of civilization. There is no tyranny [1] of our time like that which it exercises; no blinding of conscience and paralysis of will greater than that which it produces. Year after year the armies grow and the fleets expand. Year after year the war debts rise and the screw of taxation is turned mercilessly down another thread. Science is incessantly tortured in the hope of wringing from her some new death-dealing instrument, which will give one nation advantage over others. It is a race of death, spurred on by fear and hatred, in which every nation seems determined to outstrip others even at the expense of plunging headlong into the bottomless pit of exhaustion and ruin. Nearly five millions of soldiers under arms; seventeen

---

[1] Gladstone said, in a letter to a committee of the Friends in Lancashire, April 16, 1889: "Militarism is the most conspicuous tyrant of the age."

or eighteen millions more trained in the last
tactics of death; a conscriptive system holding all Europe in the grasp of its enslaving
hand, turning every able-bodied man into a
fighting machine, and effacing, for a portion
of every citizen's life, the last vestige of liberty of conscience; young men by millions
taken from home, from education, from
business, and passed through the harden-
ing, demoralizing influences of camp and
barracks, thus polluting at its very sources
the life of the next generation; a thousand
war vessels prowling about the seas; one
third of the annual revenues spent on preparations for war, and another third on wars
already fought; national debts grown to
frightful proportions (thirty thousand millions of dollars in the aggregate), and still
growing; new implements of death — magazine guns, rapid-fire guns, dynamite guns —
daily turned out, new warships launched,
new fortifications erected and manned; the
nations in perpetual jealousy, hatred and
fear, bound hand and foot by suspicion, un-

able to unite in the simplest deeds of right and justice, — such is the amazing phenomenon presented by so-called Christendom to-day![1] Talk of federation, under these circumstances, would seem, at first thought, to be fitting only for an asylum for the hopelessly insane.

The war system has so far resisted every effort to check its growth. In fact, no direct effort to check it has ever been made until recently, and none at all by the governments themselves. On the contrary, they have zealously and systematically promoted it, and the people have remained so blinded by its terrible magnificence, and so bewildered by its antiquity and supposed necessity, that they have weakly and fawningly thrown themselves under its Juggernaut wheels and allowed themselves to be crushed by millions. Of late years, the

---

[1] The annual editions of the *Statesman's Year-Book*, Hazell's *Annual* and Mulhall's *Dictionary of Statistics* may be consulted for the figures of the growth of militarism in recent years.

heads of the governments, at Christmas time, have indulged in pious effusions about peace, but at the same time they have carefully filled their powder magazines a little fuller, recommended the construction of new battleships, and added new regiments to their armies. The war system is steadily spreading its baleful influences throughout the world.[1] The nations of the Orient, just emerging from their former errors and superstitions, are, under the influence of the Western nations, turning their thought and their revenues to the creation of armies and fleets rather than to the development of the arts of civil life. This is particularly true of Japan, the progressive nation of the East, which, since the close of her war with China, has surprised and frightened the Western nations by the magnitude and rapidity of her naval extension. Our own country, abandoning its historic policy,

---

[1] In his recently published book, *The Wonderful Century*, chap. xix., Alfred Russel Wallace characterizes militarism as "the curse of civilization."

is now in the full tide of naval construction, in time of peace, and is beginning, only
half consciously as yet, but none the less
really, to vie with the nations of Europe
for naval supremacy.

There are people enough who think
that this emulous expansion of militarism
is all wrong; private citizens and public
men enough who deplore the existence of
" bloated armaments " and the crushing
burden of war taxes; friends of peace
enough in all countries who condemn as
iniquitous the whole system in general;
governments enough which upbraid all
other governments for going forward a
single step in the mad race toward what
all see will be irretrievable ruin. But here
the protest, for the most part, stops. All
is wrong in general, but everybody in particular is right — in his own eyes. There
is scarcely a man to say that *his* country
ought at once to withdraw from the wicked
rivalry. There are probably not a hundred
influential men in the United States who

will declare unequivocally that our own country ought not to build another warship ; that to continue the building up of our navy is both perilous and unworthy of our national character.   There is not a public man at Washington, so far as I know, who will dare to say this, or even allow himself to think it.   In the House of Commons in 1896, where three years before a unanimous vote in favor of arbitration had been given,[1] the friends of military retrenchment were able to muster barely thirty votes against an increase in the naval budget, and their effort found little apparent sympathy in the nation at large. On the European continent, except possibly in Italy, any public man in one of the great powers would be instantly and almost universally declared a traitor, who dared to hint that his country should stop trying to

[1] The Cremer resolution, favoring a treaty of arbitration with the United States, was passed by the House of Commons, *without a division*, on the 16th of June, 1893.

keep pace with other countries in military extension and begin single-handed the work of disarmament. The plea of necessity — the sinner's favorite plea — is everywhere made : Others do so; therefore we must do so until they do otherwise. So the barbarous system continues its tyrannous hold upon the nations. The cup of its iniquity is not yet full, it seems.

How is this gigantic, growing evil to be arrested and gotten out of the way ? Federation and peace cannot make much visible progress while the governments, with the consent and encouragement of the people, make it their chief business to cultivate the arts of estrangement and war. The largest and most serious question which can be asked to-day is, How much farther is the militarism of the civilized world to go ? Is the United States so to fall under its dominion as to build up a great fleet of five hundred war vessels, make all its seaboard cities like mediæval castles, and militarize its people by a system of forced instruction in the tactics of war? Are China and Japan to climb to the war-level — perhaps it would be more true to say descend to the war-level — of England, France, Germany and Russia? Are the nations of South and of Central America, and those just beginning to bud on the Dark Continent, to follow in the same path, until the "armed camp" of Europe becomes, fifty years hence, the armed camp of the world?

There is no end to the questions to which the dreadful situation gives rise. Is all this militarism to continue developing until the nations become so virtuous as all at once to join in simultaneous and complete or gradual disarmament? Or until the tension becomes so great as to result in a frightful cataclysm which will overwhelm the world? Or until the financial burden grows so heavy as to force the governments to stop from sheer exhaustion, or the people to rise up in revolt against the crushing slavery and demand a new order

of administration ? Is disarmament, com-
mencing, nobody knows how, as the result
of the gradual prevalence of pacific methods
of settling international disputes, to come
about by a process of gradual decay? Or
is some nation, under the inspiration of
great Christian ideas, aroused by some
grand God-sent man or men, or pushed
forward by a deep spirit of right moving
in its masses, to take the initiative, begin
disarmament alone, throwing itself for protection on God and the manhood of the
world, and thus on the high ground of love
and duty lead the nations to "beat their
swords into ploughshares and their spears
into pruning-hooks " ?

All these are serious questions. No
thoughtful mind can face the dreadful re-
ality of the growing tyranny of militarism,
as it now exists, without asking some or all
of them. Which of them, how many of
them, shall be answered in the affirmative ?
Perhaps we shall be better able, so far as
able at all, to choose among them and find

answers which shall have at least a working value, after we have examined the origin and growth of the international peace movement, — a movement which has already become so strong as to put the war system considerably on the defensive, which betokens its ultimate if not speedy overthrow and the final enthronement in the world of universal and permanent coöperation and peace.

V

The Influence of Christianity in restoring the Federative Principle

THE whole movement for the abolition of war, for the establishment of peaceful relations between men, and for the ultimate federation of all the interests of human society, began with the appearance of Christianity. The movement has, of course, a natural basis in the constitution of humanity, as heretofore stated. There are many natural forces at work in it, and these are becoming more powerful every year ; but their activity and efficiency are due, for the most part, to the quickening and liberating influence which Christianity has had upon them. Prior to the advent of Christ the elements of division and disintegration, heretofore described, rendered the natural peace forces nearly powerless, and outside of the circle of his influence they still hold practically undisputed mastery. Whatever gains were made at particular times and places in the way of concord were soon lost in the general chaos of greed, hate, violence and disorder. The influence of Christianity in setting free the peace forces of human nature and human society, and starting them into activity, has been slow and not very uniform; but it has been incessant and sure, and some of the first ripe fruit of it is just now being gathered.

This influence has been exerted through a Person, a Book and a Society. The Founder of Christianity was a perfect peacemaker. He was not directly an anti-war prince. He said and did little directly about the practice of war as it existed everywhere about him. He seems to have ignored it. His work was positive and constructive. He was the Prince of Peace, unarmed and incapable of bearing the arms of worldly warfare. All the forces which make for peace were always active in him; those which produce war found no place in his being. His speech and conduct reveal no traces of them. The sword which he came to send [1] was the sword of truth and love, which was to be drawn against all the institutions of selfish hate, in the family, in the state and in the world. The strife that he set going was that in which men conquer by patient loyalty to truth and by cheerfully allowing themselves to be killed for its sake; not that in which men draw the steel blade of violence to spill each other's blood.

Jesus Christ loved men. That was his life, his supreme motive, his only passion. He went about doing them good, in spirit and in body. There was nothing he would not do to help men; but he never did harm to any one. He lifted not a finger of violence in self-defense or in defense of others. It is impossible to conceive of him as having armed himself against his fellow-men

[1] Matthew x. 34. Compare Luke xii. 49 ff.

for any purpose whatever, or to have smitten one in the interests of another. If he used force at all, it stopped short of being hurtful.[1] Fearless, faithful to truth, unmasking unreality, but tender, patient, forgiving, harmless, loving and helpful even

[1] Dr. Lyman Abbott, in *Christianity and Social Problems*, chap. ix., adduces Christ's example in the purification of the temple, and in the garden when the soldiers of the guard fell backward to the ground, as a proof that Jesus approved of the deadly use of force in the defense of others. At least, that appears to be his conclusion, though he does not say it in so many words. It is difficult to see how the power which Jesus exercised on those two occasions is to be classed as physical force, as we use the term. It was certainly not the whip of small (straw) cords which induced any one to leave the temple. If an argument for the use of force in a punitive way is to be based on these incidents, then Christ's restraint in its employment on both occasions would certainly go to show that he meant that its use should always stop short of being deadly or really harmful. If "love may use force," as Dr. Abbott contends, it must use it in such a way as to manifest itself as "love" towards both the parties with whom it is dealing, and not towards one alone. This is really the significance of Christ's example in these and other instances.

unto death, he gave himself in total sacrifice, seeking nothing in return, that he might create in men a spirit like his own, and thus unite them to God, and to one another in a kingdom of love and mutual beneficence.   This great loving, peace-making Person, through the record left of him, has been speaking and acting in all the generations since, as no other person has done, as all other persons combined have not done.   Thought and speech for nineteen centuries have been unable to get away from him ; they are less able to get away from him to-day than ever before.   His character and example, wherever known, have appealed powerfully to men's spirits and tended to create, and actually created in greater or less degree, lives and dispositions like his own.   Who can estimate the cumulative power of such a personality on individuals, on society, on institutions ?

As with the Person, so with the Book. The New Testament [1] is the Book of

[1] The New Testament, not the Bible as a whole, is

Peace. It says little about war as an institution. But the spirit of selfishness, envy,
hate, retaliation and vengeance, out of
which war springs, is everywhere repro-
bated on its pages. It exalts love to the
supremest place among the virtues. It
makes goodwill the heart of righteousness.
Its great thesis is the Fatherhood and love
of God manifested in a practical way in
Jesus Christ. Love to God and love to
man, self-sacrifice for others, forgiveness of
injuries, non-resistance of evil with evil,
overcoming evil with good, brotherly fellowship and peace, are the foremost of its
practical teachings. On these it always in-
sists ; the opposites of these it always con-
demns. The New Testament is to-day, un-
important particulars aside, the same book
as when in collected form it was first read
to the churches in the second and third

the final standard as to Christian teaching on this subject. Those who appeal to the Old Testament to support war abandon Christian grounds. See Matthew v.
38 ff.

centuries. It has been the same in every period of Christian history. Men have turned its God and Saviour into curious likenesses of themselves, misinterpreted its doctrines, made strange travesties of its practical teachings, or omitted entirely the most essential of them. But in spite of these perversions and misinterptetations, its pages of love, goodwill and peace, ever the same, read and re-read century after century, have spoken in their natural simplicity direct to multitudes of hearts. It has been better than the best of its interpreters, and good in spite of the worst. It has thus gradually turned men's ideas into new lines, and given the world an increasingly clear conception of the true law of individual and social life, of the true relations of the societies of men, as well as of individuals, one to another.

These great principles of goodwill, mutual service and peace, taught by Christ, transmitted in the New Testament, and operating, now strongly, now feebly, in the society which he formed, have gradually permeated the life of peoples and nations, and transformed their habits of thought, their morals, customs, laws and political institutions.[1] The Christian Society, speaking of it in the large, though often far from ideal, and frequently in parts of it Christian in almost nothing but name, has been instrumental in working out the conditions of universal and lasting federation and peace chiefly through the new and profounder idea, and the better example, of kinship which it has presented. The kinship lying at the basis of Christian civilization, as its creative principle, is not the kinship of the *family*, under earthly parenthood, but the kinship of *man*, in the Fatherhood of God.[2] The kinship of the family, unless regenerated and directed by something beyond itself, tends naturally to exclusiveness, clannishness and social division. At best, the range of its cultivation of

---

[1] Charles Loring Brace, *Gesta Christi*.

[2] Benjamin Kidd, *Social Evolution*, chap. vii.

the social affections is narrow. The kinship of man in the Fatherhood of God, when truly realized, tends naturally to universal fellowship, to social union, and thus to liberty and equal rights. It recognizes no distinction of highborn and lowborn. It declares every man the brother of every other man. It ignores all lines of descent and all boundaries of nationality. It drives out hate and strips off the weapons with which selfishness had armed itself. It puts on a whole armor of goodwill and loving service.

This great Christian principle of the divine kinship of men has gone with, or rather carried, the Christian Society into all the world, across all national boundaries, over all the barriers created by caste. It has worked slowly and irregularly, it is true, and against great obstacles from within the Society and from without, but its influence on the whole has been enormous. It has caused multitudes of men in every age since the time of Christ to live together in mutual helpfulness and peace, and often to settle their disputes, if any arose, by referring them to the impartial judgment of their friends.[1] It has created a new sense of human worth and human dignity. It has undermined tyranny and slavery, not wholly yet, but in a very marked degree. It has developed democracy in government. It has set free the impulses to travel and to trade, and thus created the world-wide commercial interchanges of our day, — a system as absolutely dependent on brotherly coöperation and trust, for its normal growth and development, as religion itself. It has changed the whole notion of nationality from its former meaning of an enforced union under kingly authority, and has rebuilt it, or is fast rebuilding it, upon the principles of mutual interest and the consent of the governed. It has led gradually to the general substitution of law for violence in the adjustment of personal misunderstandings within national limits.

[1] *Gesta Christi*, chaps. viii., xii., xiii., xiv., xxvii.

It has created a system of international law, and is slowly improving it. Liberty, equality, fraternity, whose names the French revolutionists wrote with such terrible emphasis on the façades of all the public buildings of Paris, are great conceptions, — Christian, human. But fraternity is first, not last. Brotherhood is the ground principle of all our Christian civilization. Without the sense of brotherhood love would be impossible, and without this, expressing itself in manifold practical forms, the whole structure of our modern social organism, weak enough as it is, would collapse into the ancient discord, and war, which is the outward expression of selfishness and hate, would be eternal.

It is needless to say that this principle of the divine kinship of men, set forth and exemplified by Christ, taught with such directness and force in the New Testament, and operative with growing power, through the Christian Society, in the reconstruction of all human institutions, is the root from

which has sprung the modern peace movement, — the movement for the abolition of
war, and for the federation and friendly
coöperation of all the nations of the earth.

VI

War Ethically Wrong

THE movement for the abolition of war, as a distinctive phase of humane reform, has two main grounds. One of these is the conception that war *per se* is always ethically wrong; the other, that it is anti-federative, or anti-social, and therefore opposed to all the great interests of human society. According to the first of these conceptions, war is condemned because it violates not only the great law of love set forth by the Founder of Christianity, but as well every principle of the moral law; because it settles no question on the basis of right; because it is a system having no element of humanity in it; because it originates in and is supported by selfishness, hate and revenge; because its deeds are always wicked and inhuman ; because it calls out all the baser passions, is prolific of vice and crime and produces general social demoralization. From this point of view, war is held always to be unlawful as a means either of promoting good or of defense against evil, a wicked and inhuman instrument, which no group of enlightened human beings can ever innocently use against another.   This view does not maintain that no good result has ever come from any war ; it does maintain that a good end does not justify the use of an essentially evil means, even though the desired end may be reached thereby, but that the result should be brought about by a different means.   The view likewise does not maintain that war has never been relatively right for some peoples in some ages of the world ; it does maintain that, in the nature of things, from the constitution of men and their relations to God and to one another, it is fundamentally and everlastingly wrong, and that those who have come to a knowledge of its intrinsic character can never have anything to do with it, and are under the supremest obligation not only to abstain from all war themselves, but to do all in their power to bring others to see it in the same light and treat it in the same way.[1]

Historically, the peace movement, in its modern organized form, originated in this conception. The conception is as old as Christianity, and operated in the general work of Christianization long before any distinctive peace movement was thought of. No sooner had Christian men looked at the system of war from the standpoint of the character, example and teachings of Jesus and of the whole spirit of the gospel,

---

[1] For an exposition of this view, consult the *Essays on Morality*, by Jonathan Dymond; the *Manual of Peace*, by Thomas C. Upham; *The Early Christians and War*, by Thomas Clarkson; *Observations on the Distinguishing Views and Practices of the Friends* (chap. xii.), by J. J. Gurney; the *Speeches and Addresses* of John Bright; *Defensive War*, by Henry Richard. Consult also the writings of Count Leo Tolstoy, who is the most distinguished living advocate of the principle of the entire unlawfulness of war.

than the utter incompatibility of the two at once dawned on them. This was the conception and practice of the early Christians, as a whole, for more than a hundred years.[1] It was the conception of many of the leading exponents of Christianity during the second and third centuries, before the great apostasy set heavily in. Later, it was the conception of Wyclif,[2] the first light of the Reformation and of a restored primitive Christianity. It was the conception, in the seventeenth century, of George Fox[3] and William Penn, in whom and in the society formed by whom the Reformation found for a brief period its fullest ideal expression.

When the peace movement entered upon its organized existence in the early part of this century, as a definite effort to do away with war, this conception lay at the bottom

---

[1] J. Bevan Braithwaite, *The Early Christians and War*, in London Peace Congress Report.

[2] Robert Vaughan, *Life of Wyclif*, vol. ii. chap. vii.

[3] *Journal*, in various passages.

of the undertaking.[1]   The early peace
societies organized in this country from
1815 to 1828 were founded, every one of
them, by men whose minds and consciences
had gone to the bottom of the iniquity of
war and discarded it in every shape.[2]   The
London Peace Society, founded in 1816,
had the same basis.   For fifty years the
chief supporters of the propaganda were,
not wholly but mostly, "peace-at-any-price"
men, as they have been contemptuously
but falsely called.   William Allen, Thomas
Clarkson, Jonathan Dymond, Joseph John
Gurney, Richard Cobden, Joseph Sturge,
John Bright, Henry Richard, and their
faithful co-workers in Parliament and out
of it ; Noah Worcester, whose "Solemn
Review" aroused the churches of two nations ; William Ladd, the matchless Apostle

[1] Noah Worcester, *Solemn Review of the Custom of
War.*

[2] For an account of the organization of the first peace
societies, see papers by Dr. W. Evans Darby, W. C.
Braithwaite, Esq., and Benjamin F. Trueblood, in the
Report of the Chicago Peace Congress of 1893.

of Peace and first general organizer of the work,[1] whose treatise on " A Congress and Court of Nations," sixty years ago, left little to be said on the subject; Adin Ballou,[2] the distinguished founder of this lectureship, for many years president of the New England Non-Resistant Society; Thomas C. Upham,[3] William Lloyd Garrison,[4] John G. Whittier,[5] Elihu Burritt,[6] — all these were men who believed war to be essentially sinful and never justifiable, a vast system of iniquity to be dug up by the roots and cast out of human society. These were the great prophets to whom the word of the Lord came in the wilderness, whose inspired utterances aroused the sleeping conscience of the world. Others, of course,

[1] See *Memoir of William Ladd, the Apostle of Peace*, by John Hemmenway.

[2] Consult the *Autobiography of Adin Ballou*, edited by William S. Heywood.

[3] *The Manual of Peace*.

[4] Consult the *Life of Garrison*, by his Sons.

[5] See various poems on Peace and Disarmament.

[6] *Life and Labors of Elihu Burritt*.

who did not take this radical view, for example, Dr. Channing,[1] Charles Sumner,[2] Judge William Jay,[3] Dr. Peabody,[4] became hearty supporters of the cause and did it service of a very high order.   But they did not originate it.   The men who brought the movement forth, who organized the first societies, and afterwards the first international congresses,[5] who furnished the means, who cherished the cause through vituperation and ridicule into the respect which it has at last won, were peace-at-any-price men, or rather, as they should always be called, peace-on-principle men.   The movement would not have started when it did, and not even yet possibly, but for the undimmed consciences, the courage and

[1] For Channing's views, see essays on War, in his collected works.

[2] *The True Grandeur of Nations.*

[3] *Review of the War with Mexico.*

[4] *Address before the American Peace Society.*

[5] See Report of the Peace Congresses of Brussels, Paris, Frankfort, London and Edinburgh, 1848–1853, published in one volume, by the London Peace Society.

self-sacrificing devotion, of these princes of
peace.

Not much is heard nowadays of this class
of peace men, except in the way of apology
or derogation. I have recently heard it
asserted at an important peace conference
that the genus is about extinct ; that the
position has been found to be untenable
and has been abandoned. Many of those
who are seeking earnestly to promote the
principle and practice of arbitration are
careful to say that they are not peace-at-
any-price men. They even go out of their
way to say a good word for war under
certain exigencies. Their consciences are
nearer to the radical peace view than they
are willing to admit, but they feel bound
to keep up a sort of consistency with their
past, with the fighting idea of "patriotism"
and of "honor," and with an old historic
notion about war, from which they are not
quite strong enough and brave enough to
break away.

My firm and mature conviction, formed

on religious, moral and historic grounds, is that this conception of the entire unlawfulness of war, which has been held by so many Christian leaders in the past and which created the peace movement, is in no remote future inevitably to become universal among good men.   Its adherents are not decreasing.   They are more numerous throughout Christendom to-day than ever before.   Witness the hundred thousand Stundists in Russia, many of whom sympathize strongly with the opinions of Count Tolstoy; the twenty thousand Doukhobortsi[1] in the Russian Caucasus; the thirty thousand Nazarenes in southern Hungary; the Friends, Mennonites and Moravians, who still, in many parts of the world, maintain their ancient profession; the increasing number of individuals in all the

---

[1] The Doukhobortsi, for their refusal to bear arms, have recently been subjected to persecutions worthy of the most barbarous times. *Christian Martyrdom in* ·
Russia, recently published by the Brotherhood Publishing Co., Paternoster Square, London, contains an account of their persecutions and exile.

denominations who will no longer make any apology for war; the many individuals in continental Europe who refuse to do military service of any kind.[1] .

It is true, war is not attacked on this ground so exclusively as formerly. The crusade against it has become so widespread and powerful, and is pushed forward on so many strong grounds,—rational, humanitarian, social, economic, — that it seems unnecessary to put this fundamental ethical view forward so constantly as formerly. Most of those who hold it, and are ready to defend it on all proper occasions, are only too glad to join with other true

[1] Van der Ver, of Holland, whose recent heroic refusal to do military service Tolstoy has preserved for all time, is only one of an increasing body of young men in Europe whose example would be much more contagious than it is if their conduct were not so carefully kept by the authorities from the knowledge of the public. One of the leading lawyers of Brussels, a Belgian senator, told the writer in 1894 that what is needed more than anything else in Europe to-day, to break down the tyranny of militarism, is a large body of men who will refuse to do military service of any kind.

friends of the cause, on common grounds,
and to coöperate with them in the practical
effort now being made to establish permanent peaceful methods of settling all disputes. War will be abolished on these common grounds rather than on the perfect
ethical one, except so far as that mingles
with the others and gives them vitality and
persistence, as it does and always will do ;
just as the radical, immediate emancipation
principle was always the backbone of the
anti-slavery movement.   But when the hor-
rible system of human butchery shall have
been abolished, then all good men will be
"peace-at-any-price" men, just as all good
men are now anti-slavery men ; and they
will wonder then that any man of conscience could ever have been anything else.
As Victor Hugo prophesied at the open-
ing of the peace congress at Paris, in 1849,
people will then look upon a cannon in a
museum as we now look upon an instrument of torture, with amazement that such
a thing could ever have been. The "peace-

at-any-price" men will then have their complete vindication at the bar of a thoroughly christianized and enlightened public conscience. The principle out of which their opposition to war springs is the seed-principle of the whole federative movement of human society, and no one can understand the spirit and history of this movement who does not take into account the place which these men have held in it. Some of the radical advocates of peace hold that no effective opposition to war can be made by those who do not hold and practice this principle. In this, it seems to me, they are mistaken, as the discussion will presently show.

VII

War Anti-Federative

THE other leading ground on which the crusade against war is carried on is that it is anti-federative. War is now seen by all sensible men to be a huge load on the constructive forces of society, an immeasurable obstacle to the free play of the federative elements in human nature. It reduces national prosperity to a minimum, not only by wasting men, labor, money, material, intellectual activity, sentiment and moral force at home, but likewise by keeping peoples apart and preventing the profitable interaction of those federative forces, and the mutual use of those special resources of different lands, on which the moral development and common weal of the world so much depend. Under the long action of Christianity and of the natural forces which Christianity has brought more and more into healthful activity, the federative tendencies have become powerfully operative in our modern society, especially between individuals and contiguous communities, but also between nations. Witness the broad range of religious and philanthropic work, the reformatory movements, the commercial and industrial enterprises, in a word, the multitude of humane as well as profit-seeking enterprises of our day, which pay little regard to national boundaries. For this reason, war is coming to be held intolerable, and the spirit out of which it springs irrational and utterly stupid. It not only wastes and destroys the accumulations of the past ; it checks and obstructs, and often almost entirely paralyzes all federative, constructive work, without which families and communities are so helpless in these days, from almost every point of view. The peace movement has therefore drawn into it, or rather had forced into it, large numbers of men who are not yet ready to grant that war as an instrument is always morally unlawful. The great concern now is to get rid of it in the speediest way, not to prove it in every case morally wrong. By most thoughtful men, except a few whose brains are still strangely streaked with protoplasm, — men who prate about the glory of war, its inculcation of the manly virtues, its necessity to prevent civilization from decaying, — it is considered in all ordinary cases sufficiently immoral and always dreadful enough to enlist their heartiest sympathy and coöperation in every feasible effort to banish it from the world.

Some of our radical peace men have wondered at the sudden influx of men of this description — statesmen, jurists, scholars, literary men, bankers, stock exchangers, capitalists, workingmen, socialists, etc. — into the ranks of the peace forces. They have hastily inferred that the movement is getting on to lower ground. But this is only apparently so. The ground, though broader, is really the same, — the incompatibility, that is, of war with the federative nature of men, and therefore with all the great interests of mankind. If war wrought no damage to the moral and material welfare of the race, no opposition to it would ever have been made. The protest of the early peace men against war, as essentially and always immoral, grew really out of the positive conception that men and nations are so constituted that they ought to love one another; that this is the law of their being; that mutual service and coöperation are obligatory, because the different social units and groups are naturally members one of another, and cannot reach their proper development, comfort and happiness in any other way.

The protest would have been true, possibly, if there existed no federative nature in men. Aggression and revenge, fighting and mutual destruction, would be wrong if individuals and nations had absolutely no power of mutual service. But the protest would never have been made, or even thought of, or, if made, would have seemed shadowy and irrelevant, but for the positive demand in the constitution of humanity for good-will, coöperation and solidarity. Made from the standpoint of these principles, which were urged with great force by the early opponents of war,[1] the protest gradually recommended itself as essentially sound, and has had a powerful influence in awakening the already stirring conscience of the civilized world, not only to the cruelty and inhumanity of war, but also to its absurdity and entire needlessness. On the ground of these federative principles and the destructive effect of war and war preparations upon the solidarity of human interests, many have joined the peace movement who have not been able to follow the "peace-at-any-price" men to the logical conclusion of the principles. This is the explanation of the sudden development which the movement against war has recently shown throughout

[1] Noah Worcester, *The Friend of Peace*, 1815–1827.

the civilized world. The movement is not
getting on to lower ground. It is on the
same ground, essentially, and is gradually
drawing into it all those in whom the Christian progress of the world has created a
sincere and often large love for human
good, for practical human brotherhood.
The movement is therefore immensely
stronger, because of the number of its adherents, and the power which it thereby
possesses to secure practical results in legislation, than it was when it had no friends
except the radical ones, who spent their
time largely in depicting the horrors and
revolting cruelties of the battlefield, and in
collating and expounding texts of the New
Testament to prove their one thesis, that
war, defensive as well as offensive, is always
unlawful. The federative tendencies and
beliefs of the larger number of men of
what are sometimes called half-and-half
principles, who have in recent years given
their support to peaceful methods of settling disputes, have made possible the ex-

cellent results which have been attained both in the field of international arbitration and in that of industrial arbitration. All of the statesmen[1] who have done so much in this century in securing the adjustment of international disputes by peaceful methods have been men who would not have hesitated, under given circumstances, to go to war. How much more might have been done, if these men had all been radical peace men, it is useless to try to conjecture. But one thing is certain : without their cordial belief in arbitration and the spirit out of which it springs, nothing at all would yet have been accomplished in a practical way.

[1] I am not arguing that these men are nearer right than the radical peace men, but only that the movement has become immensely stronger since so many of them

---

[1] Jay, Jefferson, Pinkney, Webster, Grant, Gladstone, Sumner, Fish, Schenck, Earl Grey, Sir S. H. Northcote, Sir E. Thornton, Rose, Count Sclopis, Staempfli, Blaine, Pauncefote, Gresham, Olney, Foster, and others.

have interested themselves in it, and that
the ground of their support is, as far as it
goes, true peace ground. The old thesis I
believe to be profoundly right. Its constant
maintenance was absolutely necessary in
its time. Men's minds were so stupefied
by false ideas about the glory and the necessity of war that only the most intense
radicalism and realism of treatment could
arouse them. Only radical men would have
ventured into the halls of legislation, in the
early days, with memorials to urge the
claims of peaceful methods in composing
international troubles. The maintenance of
the thesis is still necessary as an essential
part, nay, rather, the very centre and core,
of the peace movement. There are times
when radical peace men are the only peace
men left, all others being carried away by
the spirit of war. In Russia, where this
thesis is maintained with so much vigor and
freshness by Tolstoy, supported by multitudes of peasants throughout the empire,
the peace propaganda cannot yet take on

any other form. The great count is toler-
ated only because it is known by the state
authorities that he will not take up arms,
and that he counsels others not to take up
arms, against the government. Thus he
and his followers are doing for Russia what
men of no other principles could do. It is
felt by a number of the friends of peace in
Europe that the yoke of European militarism can never be broken until there
arise in the midst of it a body of men who
will refuse, for conscience' sake, to do military service in any form.

But, after all, the real strength of the
peace movement does not lie in the protest against war and its desolations, cruelties and horrors. It lies in the *protest for
concord*, and its utilities and glories. The
former is only a part of the latter. Men
can never be brought to see the wickedness
of violence until they see the true nature of
peace on its positive side, the moral grandeur of love, the individual and social worth
of cordial fellowship, the immense economic

and happiness value of wide-reaching industrial and commercial coöperation, the in-
calculable benefits, the dignity and honor-
ableness of international trust and concord.
Men who do not see these will, as a rule,
never see anything wrong in war. When
they see these, you will not need to portray
to them the moral hideousness of war.
For war and war preparations are nothing
but the outward manifestation of the spirit
of exclusiveness, hate, greed and aggression on the part of nations. When this
spirit goes out of men, war and war preparations go out of them. So long as this
spirit remains, it is idle to talk of disarmament. You can do something, especially
among thinking Christian men, to create
a new feeling about war by holding it up
to the shafts of a pitiless moral analysis,
but you can do much more among the
masses of men, to whom fine ethical conceptions do not so much appeal, by showing that war is the deadly enemy of all
those economic and social interchanges on

which the prosperity, the happiness and the moral welfare of peoples of all lands now so largely depend. This is the ground on which much of the most effective peace work is now being done. Still more can be done by setting in movement, or by aiding in developing, all sorts of healthy international coöperation.

VIII

The New World Society

THE main ground of hope at the present time for the speedy abolition of war is, not some theoretical guess as to what the federative forces ought to do or may do, but their actually existing results in the social, economic and political structure of the world, constituting a world society of very marked development. This world society may be traced in many directions. Christian missions, in an organized and permanent form never known until this century, now have their growing centres of religious and educational activity in every quarter of the globe,[1] and Christ's doctrine of the brotherhood of men in the Father-

[1] F. Max Müller, *Lecture on Missions.* Theodore Christlieb, *Protestant Foreign Missions.* James S. Dennis, *Christian Missions and Social Progress.*

hood of God was never set forth with so
much simplicity, directness, freedom from
prejudice, and practical efficiency as in the
present generation.

(Following these missions and in part created by them, commerce has grown and
spread until it has become world-wide. It
has woven its network of intercourse, and
planted the homes of its merchants and car-
riers on the shores of all the continents and
of the important islands of the sea, and
pushed itself into the heart of the most unknown inlands. It has discovered new resources, opened up new occupations, taught
workingmen to go from one end of the earth
to the other. It has created a great credit
system, which is fast uniting all the large
cities of the world and many smaller ones
together in a community of interest.

Labor has not only its national, but also
its international associations, which are
bringing the millions of laboring people in
many lands into ever closer union and sympathy, and the working classes have already

learned that they have a higher mission than to be the mere tools of capital or of selfish and greedy monarchs. There is no federative force more powerful than that of labor, and it is binding society together at the very bottom.

International travel, not for religious and commercial purposes only, but also for intellectual, scientific and social purposes, has been rendered swift and easy by the inventions which have led to the formation of the great steamship lines and the transcontinental railways. The volume of travel merely for sight-seeing and pleasure, for rest and recuperation, has become so immense that for three months in each year it seems as if the whole civilized world were in migration.[1]

This internationalization of religion, of business, of society, of science, etc., by ac-

[1] During the recent war with Spain many of the steamship lines between the United States and Europe found their business cut down nearly fifty per cent. What this means in checking the natural flow of money throughout the world is easily imagined.

quainting peoples with one another, is removing many prejudices, and teaching men
the numerous ways in which those remotest
from one another may contribute to one
another's prosperity and happiness. The
telegraph, the cable and the associated
press have put all parts of this complex
world structure into almost instant contact
with one another, so that a disturbance in
one part is at once felt everywhere else.
This immense network of interests, all an-
tagonistic to war, is constantly being woven
thicker and firmer; the result of it will be,
in the near future, that the world society,
purely in self-defense, will banish war from
its midst, as a necessary condition of the
permanence of the federation and union of
interests in which each unit finds its life
and well-being.) Formerly, when the nations
traded little with each other, when their
citizens sojourned little abroad, when international communication was slow and difficult,[1] when property was in the hands of

[1] It was several days before the knowledge of the

a few lords, and the people were menials and knew little of the real comforts and blessings of life, two nations might fight and desolate each other, for a series of years even, and the rest of the nations feel it little or care little about it, except from the military standpoint of the rulers, who were glad oftener than not, because of the opportunity for exploits which the wars of neighboring states opened to them.   In our time, a war between two nations is, in its effects at least, a war everywhere.   Every nation's industry and commerce are crippled; every nation's credit disturbed; every nation's citizens imperiled; every nation's happiness and comfort interfered with.

In this complex state of international society, and because of the awful destructiveness of modern implements of warfare, it is inevitable that there should soon be some concert of the nations to reduce war, when it occurs, to the briefest possible period, to

battle of Waterloo, in 1815, got across the Channel and reached London.

the narrowest limits, and ultimately to prevent it entirely.   This concert is likely to
be for a time in part a concert of force,
exerting itself in the neutralization [1] of small
countries, in the protection of commerce on
the high seas, and in preventing any nation
from breaking the peace.   But the concert
of force, which from its very nature can be
participated in by only a few great powers,
contains in it so many elements of danger,
and is, from the very selfishness out of
which it springs, so liable to break down at
the critical moment, as it did in the case of
the recent Armenian massacres, that the
conscience of the world will not be satisfied
very long with such an arrangement.   The
world society must have something of a
higher order, a moral concert founded in
mutual beneficence and trust.   The concert
of force, while it grows, and so long as it
lasts, is likely, too, to be limited to those
nations where militarism has come up from

[1] T. K. Arnoldson, *Pax Mundi*, chapter on " Neu-
trality."

the past, and will probably never be entered
into by a nation of the truly modern spirit
like the United States.   At least, it is to
be hoped that it will not. The concert
which is to end war, which is even now
working itself out on a grand scale in the
movements of the world society, is to be one
of unarmed, trustful coöperation, — a force
more powerful to hold in check the demon
of violence than all the combined steel-clad
ships that ever furrowed the ocean.[1]

The antagonism to war, produced by the
various causes just mentioned, is greatly
intensified by the enlarging sympathy between peoples created by the growth of
popular government in this century.   Even
in Europe, where as yet there are only two
republics, constitutional government has

[1] An example of the kind of concert here meant is
found in the Universal Postal Union. This union,
which originated no longer ago than in 1865, at its congress at Washington in 1897 admitted into its member-
ship the last of the organized nations of the world, and
became literally universal, — the first universal, international union ever formed.

made such progress that most of the sovereigns are no longer rulers except in name. (Democracy as naturally creates sympathy and the spirit of coöperation between peoples as absolutism in government is the deadly foe of international friendship.) It may take a republic like France a good while to throw off the effects of the absolutism of the past. The full influence of democracy in creating international sympathy ought not to be expected to be seen in a single generation or even in a single century, after so many centuries of absolutism have stamped their effects on the character of all peoples. In the United States, where absolutism has been unknown since the founding of the nation(sympathy with other peoples (this does not mean with other *governments*) is very large and steadily growing.) In France the spirit of the people is moving steadily into sympathy with the people of other constitutional countries, as the republic becomes more sure to maintain a permanent existence. (The peoples

of the South and Central American republics have even more sympathy one with another across the borders than the citizens
of any one of these republics have with
their own fellow-citizens, civil wars being
more common among them than international wars.) Though democracies now and
then break out into war with great passion,
against other peoples, or rather against the
governments of other peoples, this must
not be taken as invalidating the position
that popular government is naturally con-
ducive to international friendship. These
fits of international violence are not charge-
able to democratic principles, nor do they
indicate that governments of the people
have no tendency to prevent international
ill feeling and strife. They only prove that
even the best political institutions cannot
suddenly remove *in toto* deep-seated prejudices, perverted habits of thought and long-
felt dislikes and animosities. That popular
governments naturally tend to create opposition to war is sufficiently clear from the

fact that in those countries where the people have most to do with political affairs, there opposition to war is strongest and most pronounced.[1] The notion of popular government is a constituent element in the new world society whose antagonism to war is growing to be so marked. It will be seen later that the idea of the people governing themselves has even a wider bearing than that which appears in international sympathy; that it is working out a veritable world government which is some day to embrace in its jurisdiction all the nations of the earth, or humanity as a whole.

In this connection one other thought deserves mention. It seems to me that the sense of a common manhood, of a common brotherhood, revealed through citizenship which possesses the franchise, or seeking to reveal itself through such citizenship, is more the cause of the present widespread opposition to war among organizations of

[1] Andrew Carnegie, *Triumphant Democracy*, chap. xvii.

laboring men than the mere desire not to
have regular employment and steady living
wages interfered with, powerful as this latter is as a motive. (At any rate, the opposition to war on the part of democracies and
constitutional governments and the antagonism of the labor interests to militarism
move steadily and powerfully together.[1])

[1] For a careful discussion of the labor opposition to
war, see the speeches of Professor John B. Clark of
Columbia University, in the Mohonk Arbitration Conference Reports for 1896–97–98.

IX

The Growing Triumph of Arbitration

O one can understand the recent sudden development of interest in arbitration, not only in the United States and Great Britain, but also in many of the continental European countries, without taking into account this complex, economically sensitive and growingly humane and Christian condition of our modern world society. Arbitration has an interesting history of a hundred years, during which it has been successfully applied in more than a hundred important cases of difficulty.[1] But it is not primarily its past

[1] *Success of Arbitration*, pamphlet issued by the American Peace Society. *The Arbitrations of the United States*, by John Bassett Moore. *International Arbitration, its Present Status and Prospects*, by Benjamin F. Trueblood.

success which has created the recent en-
larged interest in it. In fact, the new interest in it has set many intelligent people
to work to hunt up its history, of which
they previously knew practically nothing.
(What has created the fresh interest is the
absolute moral and material necessity of
arbitration both as a means of avoiding the
widespread ruin which war now produces,
and as an expression of the increased con-
scientiousness, reasonableness and forbearance of men in regard to their differences
and their growing disposition to coöperate,
wherever possible, for mutual benefit. It
is the resistless logic of modern humane
progress which is bringing arbitration into
such esteem. This method of composing
disputes is not merely a product, but an
integral part of the great federative movement of our day, some of whose leading
features have been mentioned. Every part
of this movement has had essentially the
same causes, and every part has had a stim-
ulating and supporting effect upon every
other part.

The treaty of arbitration between the
United States and Great Britain, signed at
Washington on the 11th of January, 1897,
the vast significance of which cannot yet
be fully appreciated, is scarcely more an
expression of the great change in public
sentiment as to peace and war than it is of
the radically new spirit now beginning to
actuate diplomacy. But for this new spirit
in diplomacy, which dates particularly from
the time of the Geneva Red Cross Convention of 1864,[1] this treaty would have been
an impossibility. It is difficult to say
whether diplomacy has done more for the
promotion of public opinion in connection
with this treaty or the latter for the development of the former. Anglo-American
diplomacy has been for a hundred years
more than abreast of Anglo-American public sentiment on the subject of arbitration,
and the signing of this treaty has already
developed public sentiment on both sides
of the water in a most remarkable degree.

[1] *Encyclopædia Britannica*, " Geneva Convention."

The peace societies themselves, which have in recent years multiplied with such rapidity,[1] right in the midst of European bayonets even, and are devoting their attention largely to the promotion of arbitration as a permanent method of settling international controversies, are the creation of the same forces which brought arbitration into existence. Twenty years before the first peace society was organized, the Jay treaty between Great Britain and this country had provided for the settlement of three disputed questions by mixed commissions, — a form of tribunal which has since developed into the temporary arbitration court, which has done so much in recent years to preserve and promote the peace of the civilized world. In 1814, still a year before the organization of any peace societies, the treaty of Ghent provided for the settlement

[1] There are now about four hundred peace associations, including branch societies, in European countries. Most of these have been organized since the Paris Peace Congress of 1889.

of three further disputes by mixed commissions. This fact does not in any way
lessen the merit of the peace associations.
Though they did not create the arbitration
movement, and are only one of the many
agencies which are developing it, yet they
were its first prophets, giving the necessity
of it the first clear and positive utterance.
They have been its stanchest and steadi-
est friends. Up to the present time not
a single resolution favoring arbitration has
ever been introduced or voted on in 'any
parliament that was not there directly by
their agency.

Among the peace society agencies must
be included the International Peace Congress, a permanent organization since 1889,
meeting annually in the different large
cities of the world ; the Interparliamentary
Peace Union,[1] a distinguished association

[1] The Interparliamentary Peace Union was organized
at the time of the Paris Exposition in 1889, partly by
the same men who originated the International Peace
Congress. The union now has about fifteen hundred
members.

of members of parliaments, now having many hundreds on its roll; the International Peace Bureau at Berne;[1] and certain special conferences, like that now held annually at Lake Mohonk, N. Y., and the national conference on arbitration held at Washington in April, 1896.

But though very powerful and efficient, and increasingly so as the number of the associations increases from year to year, the peace society agency has been only one of the large group of agencies — religious, juridic, political, diplomatic, social, commercial, financial — which have, severally and jointly, pushed arbitration to the front as the only rational method of removing controversies after direct negotiation has failed.

The merits and practicability of arbitration need no longer be pleaded. It has already won its case at the bar of international public opinion. Beginning in a tentative way with the United States and

[1] The Peace Bureau was established by vote of the Peace Congress at Rome in 1891.

Great Britain a hundred years ago, it has
been applied with increasing frequency, in
recent years particularly, to disputes of
nearly every conceivable kind. The cases
which it has disposed of have ranged all
the way from those involving damages
claims of a few thousands of dollars to those
more serious controversies, touching terri-
torial limits and transgression against national rights, which have cut deeply the
national pride and sense of honor, and given
rise to hot and long-continued diplomatic
debate. Wherever it has been employed
it has succeeded. There is not a real ex-
ception to be noted. The cases which it
has settled have stayed settled. Not even
the ghost of such a case has ever arisen to
disturb anybody's tranquillity. It has been
tried by thirty-one nations, great and small,
in the Old World and the New, the United
States and Great Britain leading, the former
with about half the whole number of cases,
the latter with nearly one third.[1]

[1] Benjamin F. Trueblood, "The United States,

Arbitration has not yet wholly succeeded in preventing wars, and may not for some time yet, but its record, in the hundred years since it first came into use, is a most remarkable one, and some day, when the history of human progress begins to be really written, this record will constitute a very instructive chapter. The advantages of this method of treating disputes are so great and so apparent to all thoughtful people that, having already been so successfully tried in such a variety of cases, it is sure speedily to become more and more general. (Arbitration gives time for passion to cool. It affords opportunity to hunt up all the facts in a given case, an ignorance or one-sided knowledge of which is often the chief cause of irritation. It costs a mere pittance compared with war. It carries questions of right and justice to the forum of reason, where only they can be determined according to their merits. True

Great Britain and International Arbitration," in the *New England Magazine*, March, 1896.

honor is always vindicated before its tribunals. It leaves no bitter ranklings behind, no broken families, no devasted lands, no international feuds. It appeals to the better instincts of peoples. It removes prejudices and misjudgments. It creates sympathy and fellowship. Arbitration is not simply a cool and heartless method of disposing of difficulties; in its deeper significance it is a method of coöperation in promoting the true interests of the nations in their relations to one another. It not only peacefully composes their differences; it trains them as well in moral judgment and moral self-control. It makes their diplomacy more intelligent, more patient, more altruistic, and thus makes serious disputes much less likely to arise. A great arbitration like that of the Alabama dispute or of the Bering Sea seal question settles a whole group of international principles, and thus permanently advances international law.) The Bering Sea case is a conspicuous example of the tendency of arbitration to produce peaceful coöperation for the removal of troubles which not even an arbitral court may be able to reach. For these reasons arbitration, through the spirit out of which it springs and which it greatly develops and strengthens, will gradually remove the necessity of employing it at all, and will thus prove a powerful instrument in promoting the federation of the world.   —

The great question now in connection with this mode of settling differences is to make it permanent, to build it into a judicial system universally recognized and accepted by all the civilized nations.[1]   To-

[1] See the Memorial of the New York State Bar Association, *Mohonk Arbitration Conference Report for 1896*, Appendix B, and the speeches given in the Report. See, also, *International Tribunals*, by Dr. W. Evans Darby. Lord Chief Justice Russell, in his address at Saratoga before the American Bar Association in 1896, gives the grounds why, in his judgment, temporary tribunals are preferable to a permanent one. An excellent reply to his argument will be found in the speech of Mr. Walter S. Logan at the Mohonk Arbitration Conference in June, 1898.

ward the accomplishment of this all the agencies of peace are turning. (A hundred years is long enough to have successfully experimented. A hundred important cases, with many minor ones, settled in this way, and settled, every one of them, effectually and finally, are proof enough that the method is perfectly suited to the need, and capable of practically universal application. Permanent treaties of arbitration, providing for the setting up of a permanent tribunal, are the great desideratum of our complex, sensitive civilization. All disputes between the civilized nations ought forever hereafter, by their own sovereign and united determination, to be taken out of the realm of passion, caprice and violence, and brought within the domain of reason and law, as disputes between individuals have been. The reasons for the former are even more weighty than for the latter, and nothing but a false and silly sentimentalism stands in the way. The administrators of governments have much less ground for friction

between them than do individuals in the
private walks of life. The populations of
the nations have still less ground for enmity toward one another. International
hostilities are the most needless and wicked
of all hostilities. One can account for the
rashness and even levity with which they
are entered into, only on the ground of an
almost total absence of thoughtfulness in
regard to the real nature of international
strife, both on the part of the government
leaders and of the mass of citizens. The
procedure of the heads of governments, in
case of disputes, ought to be so prescribed
as to leave them no opportunity for caprice
or ambitious self-assertion, or for carrying
away the unthinking masses into senseless
war flurries by insidious appeals to passion
and national pride. If this were done, if
arbitration were established, under treaty
obligations, as a permanent principle of
international law, instead of being difficult
to carry out in practice, as many suppose,
it would, in my judgment, be found to be

incomparably easy, —{much easier than the administration of the common law among individuals, where there is constant friction from close contact.}

Just here lies the true significance of the Anglo - American treaty recently drawn.[1] This treaty was not needed to prevent the two nations from going to war. They are not likely ever to do that again, treaty or no treaty. They have fought but once, they have arbitrated eighteen times, since they became separate nations over one hundred years ago. This treaty is a declaration to the world that they have found arbitration not only just and honorable, but easy and pleasant, and that they believe it is safe to take the last obstacle out of its way and make it as easy as a fixed law of nature. Whatever obstacles the treaty is

[1] This treaty was signed by Richard Olney and Sir Julian Pauncefote on the 11th of January, 1897. It failed of ratification in the Senate, when the final vote was taken, on the 5th of May. The vote, counting pairs, was 50 to 30, a two thirds majority being required for ratification.

meeting with in the Senate, and however tentative and imperfect the method which it prescribes may be supposed to be, what the great body of Americans and Englishmen think of arbitration, which the treaty proposes to set up as a rule of law between them, is that it is the right mode of settling all their differences, and at the same time a perfectly simple and easy one. When it is once settled and in force, no one with Anglo-Saxon blood in his veins will be any more willing to part with it than with the railroad, the steamship, or the telegraph; and it will, in all probability, stop the clamorous mouth of war forever wherever the English tongue is spoken. The example will be contagious, and in a generation or two, if one may judge from the rapidity with which the arbitration movement is gaining strength in Europe, the entire civilized world will have set up for itself a permanent system of peaceful judicial settlement for disputes of every kind arising between the different nations. If the

Olney-Pauncefote treaty should fail of ratification in the Senate,[1] the effect will be merely to retard slightly or possibly to deflect from its most natural course the movement, but not in any way to seriously weaken or permanently check it. The forces whose working led to the negotiating of this treaty are so many and so strong that the final triumph of arbitration is as sure as the continuance of civilization. We may not be able to say just when or where, or in what manner, its great final triumph will begin, but of the certainty of that triumph in no remote future there can no longer be any reasonable doubt. When

---

[1] This lecture was given while the treaty was still under discussion in the Senate. Public sentiment in favor of such a treaty is stronger in both nations now than it was at the date of the signing of the treaty.

It is very interesting to notice, in this connection, that within a little more than a year after the defeat of the Olney-Pauncefote treaty, a similar though better general treaty of arbitration was negotiated and *ratified* by the governments of Italy and the Argentine Republic, the first of its kind to go into effect.

a permanent system of arbitration is once
in operation among the civilized nations,
there will be little difficulty in extending
it to the still uncivilized quarters of the
globe.

X

The United States of the World

AFTER arbitration, what? The advice of "Punch," "Don't never prophesy onless you know," is most excellent, but it is not very easy to follow. Every man of love and goodwill has something of the prophetic gift in him, and must make his forecast of the outcome of the processes in whose final victory he believes.

Arbitration is not the highest attainment of which humanity is capable and which it is destined to reach. Arbitration is, as Goldwin Smith says,[1] at least in one aspect of it, "a litigious, not a friendly process, and is apt to leave heartburnings in the

---

[1] See article on "The Arbitration Treaty" in *The Independent*, March 25, 1897.

nation against which the award is given."
Though all that I have said of the advantages of arbitration is true, yet the arbitration stage is one of very imperfect coöperation, where there is still friction, undue self-assertion, distrust and more or less estrangement. Beyond it is a stage where love and trust shall everywhere prevail, and all the nations' good shall be each nation's rule. We have even now a prophecy of this better stage which is to be reached in the relations of nations to one another. There are already multitudes of people in our civilized society who live, in their relations to one another, on a plane entirely beyond that of arbitration. They have nothing to arbitrate or to carry to the courts of law, because they either have no differences, or settle such as they have by the exercise of their own wits tempered with a little patience and mutual forbearance. All their ordinary dealings with one another — commercial, social, religious — are in a most real sense coöperative. This

class of persons is increasing continually, and they are paying less and less attention to national boundaries. The inevitable outcome of this sort of living among men in the same nation, and between men of different nations, will be the breaking down of international friction, the gradual disappearance of differences between nations, and the final evolution of international society to a state in which even arbitration will be practically unknown.

In the movement toward this higher state, two momentous results will follow quickly the adoption by the civilized world of a general permanent system of arbitration, namely, the reduction of armaments and a larger and more generous international coöperation. It is not easy to answer the questions raised in a former part of this discussion as to how the "bloated armaments" of the civilized world are to be gotten rid of. But arbitration is certainly to be the chief mediating agency in preparing the way for their removal. It has already done much in pointing the way. While a system of arbitration is being worked out, by the slow process of historic growth, by negotiation and treaty stipulations, these armaments are sure to grow further both in extent and in burdensomeness, bringing for a brief time practically the whole world under their heartless tyranny. At least, everything at the present time points that way; though one cannot say what unforeseen event may come about of such a nature as suddenly to change the course which things seem likely to take. In spite of my optimism and much against my wish, the conviction has grown upon me that our own country, as well as others, is for a season to fall more and more under the curse of militarism, as it fell once, contrary to all the principles of its Constitution, under the black and blighting curse of slavery. The people are still only half awake to the insidiousness of the war spirit. The law of animosity and distrust has its charms. for many of them. The blare and blaze of the great military establishments of the Old World furnishes powerful enticements to the spirit of a young and mighty people which has not yet had experience of the ruinous and degrading influences of military tyranny. Many in high places believe, or pretend to believe, that a nation cannot be great without fighting, without sacrificing thousands of its sons on the battlefield, without exhibiting an irritable and haughty spirit toward some supposed enemy, and venting its wrath in deeds of blood. This evil seed in the nation is sure to bring forth its deadly harvest unless the people can be awakened speedily from their slumber.[1]

But when arbitration has at last come into general and permanent use throughout the civilized world, as there is every reason to believe that it will after a generation or

[1] Since the above was written, the war with Spain has been fought, and the disposition of the nation to enter upon a policy of military and naval expansion is much stronger than it was before. See the reports of the Secretary of the Navy and the Secretary of War for 1898.

two, then these great military establishments with all their abominations will come
to an end. The end of them may come
suddenly, as the result of a great war, or a
series of great wars, the disastrous results
of which will be so deeply and universally
felt that the nations will never again permit
militarism to take root and grow. The end
is more likely to come by a. process of
neglect and natural decay, when arbitration,
universally adopted, shall have made the
uselessness of such war preparations, as
well as their wickedness and folly, manifest.
It is more likely still to come through simultaneous and gradual disarmament, entered
upon by voluntary agreement, and possibly
in connection with the adoption of some
general system of arbitration.[1]

[1] A good deal of light has been thrown upon the way
in which disarmament is likely to come about by the
invitation given on the 24th of August, 1898, by the Czar
of Russia, to all the powers represented at St. Petersburg, to unite in an international conference for the
discussion of the subject of a reduction of armaments
and the promotion of universal peace. This rescript of

After this great consummation, the federative forces, freed from the immense restraint which militarism has put upon them and supported by the vast energies and resources now consumed on destructive agencies, will work out the unity of humanity in less time than the most hopeful of us dare to imagine. This unity will ultimately, in the very nature of the case, be not only moral, social and economic, but political as well. The nature of man, the common interests of peoples, the great currents of Christian and humane influence, the social, industrial and political movements of our time, the new modes of travel and intercommunication, the development of inter-

Nicholas II. evidently opens a new era in the treatment of the subject of war. It brings the matter once for all into the sphere of practical politics. The conference which he has proposed seems assured, as all the powers represented at the Czar's court have, some of them with reservations, signified their approval, and their purpose to send delegates. The text of this remarkable document, given out by Count Muravieff, Russian Minister of Foreign Affairs, on the 24th of August, 1898, is given in full in the Appendix.

national law, the increasing international
coöperation through diplomacy, conferences,
commissions and arbitral boards, all fore-
shadow a complete political unity of the
world, a great international world state, built
up somewhat on the pattern of our union
of States, with supreme legislative, judicial
and executive functions touching those interests which the nations have in common.
The reasons for such an over-state, constituted of all the nations, are precisely the
same as for a federal union of local governments extending over a wide territory, like
our own republic.

These reasons will readily occur to any
thoughtful mind. The unification of law
and its administration is among the first.
Many consider the setting up of the Supreme Court to have been the chief triumph
in the Constitution of the United States.
The world needs a supreme tribunal to take
international law out of the chaotic and re-
proachful state in which it now is and bring
it up to something like the level of muni-

cipal law in the civilized nations. To this end it would seem that a parliament or legislative corps of some kind would be necessary also, and likewise a common executive.

Not less important a reason for a world state is the removal of friction and the danger of war by the creation of a feeling of unity in a common organization. One can easily imagine what the history of the United States would have been if they had become simply States without any common governmental tie. If the union of local governments in a national organization has done so much to remove friction and causes of war in the United States, in Great Britain, in France, in Italy, in Germany, what might not be expected in this regard from a union including them all ?

A third reason for an international government is the ease and inexpensiveness with which, under such an arrangement, the common interests of the nations could be treated and adjusted. If the United States and Canada, for instance, in addition to their

independent local governments, were each
connected with a wider government, charged
with the duty of looking after the interests
common to the two governments, — the
seal question, the fisheries question, the
border immigration question, — the mutual trade relations between the Canadian
people and our own would long since have
disappeared from the forum of discussion.
At present many subjects of international
concern — subjects of real importance —
get little or no attention ; and if they are
taken up, they are often treated in such a
narrow, selfish way by the governments interested that frequently for years they are
more and more confused by diplomatic sub-
tlety, until passion becomes hot, and the
nations are compelled, in order to get out
of the muddle, either to fight or to resort
at last to a little common sense. It is just
here that is found the strongest reason for
an over-state. These neglected interests,
gathering everywhere on the borders of
states as now organized, and interfering

with the normal development of the world society which is so rapidly creating itself, will as inevitably compel the establishment of a general world government as did the neglected mutual interests of the thirteen American colonies force the setting up of the United States general government, or those of the German states the German Empire.

Along what lines the movement toward this general world government will take place it is not easy tô forecast, except in a general way. Two or three courses are open, any one or all of which may be followed. The United States of America may in time become really such. The very name seems to be prophetic. Canada, Mexico and Central America may some day, of their own accord, ask to be admitted into a federal union with the United States. In time a great South American republic of republics may be formed, through some movement or groups of movements akin to that already taking place

among the Central American states and
the British Australian colonies. Then may
follow a federation of the two American continents. The United States of Europe, so
long dreamed of and written of by European
reformers,[1] seems to-day but the shadow of
a name; but whoever remembers the history of the consolidation of France, or Italy,
or Germany, or the still more remarkable
history of the consolidation of the Swiss
cantons composed of peoples of different
races, speaking different languages, into a
coherent national federation, will not say
that a United States of Europe is an impossibility. On the contrary, the whole
course of the modern history of nation-
building foreshadows a European federa-

---

[1] The late Charles Lemonnier of Paris, president for
many years of the International League of Peace and
Liberty, was one of the chief promoters of the idea of a
United States of Europe. The league still issues, at
Berne, its monthly organ, under the title of *Les Etats-
Unis d'Europe*. See "The United States of Europe,"
by Edward Everett Hale, in *The Old and New* for
March, 1871.

tion. The continent of Asia may some day have a like transformation; and that of Africa, too, renewed at last by a Christian civilization; and that of Australia before either of them, if one may judge from the federative tendencies already showing themselves between the colonies there.

If this should prove to be the way in which the world state is to work itself out, the islands of the sea will group themselves in with the continental federations where they naturally belong. At last these continental federations will flow together into a great world federation, the final political destiny of humanity, where all the larger hopes of love and fellowship, of peace and happy prosperity lie.

I do not pretend to assert that the actual order of movement will be as here outlined, but only that this is a possible, perhaps a probable order in which the federation of the world will come, at least in part. This forecast is in harmony with actual historic processes now working, and having for generations worked, at several points in civilized society.

Another course is possible. A great racial federation, as of the Anglo-Saxon people, may come first, with its centres of agglomeration in all parts of the world, which will gather to itself by an irresistible moral gravitation all other peoples. Racial federation is already playing its part very powerfully in the processes of civilization. Several races, it is true, are exhibiting, in greater or less degree, kindred phenomena. But racial distinctions are in many respects beginning to break down, because of the intermingling of peoples in all quarters of the globe. What may be styled the universal human characteristics, those belonging to the one race of man lying at the basis of all sub-races, are destined thus more and more to come to the front as against those which have marked off one portion of mankind from another. That race, whichever it may prove to be, which develops these general human characteris-

tics most fully and most rapidly, and throws
off most completely all that is adventitious
and unessential, will, in the nature of the
case, prove to be the nucleus or furnish the
nuclei about which civilization in all parts
of the world will crystallize.   Men will not
care at last by what racial name they are
called, or what language they speak, provided their highest interests of every kind
are served.   They will feel it more noble
to be men and to speak the one universal
language of men than to be Englishmen or
Germans or Frenchmen, and to speak any
of these great tongues.   Whatever race
shall prove itself fittest to lead in this federative process, whether the Anglo-Saxon,
as now seems possible, or some other, will
itself be modified, purified and strength-
ened for its work as the final world race
by what it receives from the races which it
draws to itself, and even from those which
through weakness shall finally be eliminated.

The objections which may be brought,
from the point of view of climate, against

the possibility of a world race, with more uniformity of characteristics than is found in the races as they now exist, are not so serious as might at first glance be supposed. The ease and rapidity with which men now travel, the expansion of ocean traffic, — one might almost say of ocean habitation, — and the growing habit, on the part of multitudes of families, of living a part of the time in one quarter of the globe and a part in another, make it at least not inconceivable that the time may come when there shall be much less difference in vigor and enterprise between the inhabitants of the tropics and of the temperate zones than there is to-day. Climate itself is probably in this indirect way to be one of the conquests of the coming humanity. Men will come more and more to be inhabitants of all the climates, shifting their abodes quickly from place to place, living on the seas, as an increasing number now do, and thus getting the best out of all parts of the world, while escaping with increasing certainty the weakening influences of any particular part. It is doubtless true, as Mr. Kidd argues,[1] that for a long time to come the tropics will have to be developed and in some manner and measure controlled by the people inhabiting the temperate regions. But it is difficult to believe that the rich tropical regions are always to be vassal, that their inhabitants are to remain permanently incapable of self-development and self-control. The new world race which is in process of building, by transformation, absorption and elimination, will make the matter of the inhabitancy and self-development and control of the tropics very different from what it is to-day.

It is scarcely necessary to state that this process of racial expansion, absorption and federation will, if it goes to the extent which now seems probable, result ultimately in the selection or creation of a single language for universal use. Even now the

[1] See his recently published book, *The Control of the Tropics.*

growing intercourse of different peoples is forcing upon attention the necessity of a universal language, and various schemes for the creation or selection of a language for universal use have been devised. But a universal language cannot be artificially created; it presupposes and requires a universal people.

The process of racial federation here outlined seems to me likely to play even a more important part in the development of the world state than that of simple geographical federation, though both are quite certain to work together.

It is not unlikely that the process of federation, whether it go on in one or both of the ways above indicated, will for some time to come not be entirely unattended by the incidents of war. One could wish that it might be otherwise. The federative forces and processes are in their nature pacific and opposed to the methods of war. They will ultimately make war impossible. But in the present confused movements of society, in the actual relations of nations, small and great, weak and strong, to one another, there is so much of ambition and animosity, so much of ignorance and short-sightedness, intermingled with the operations of the elements of good, that progress toward social and political unity is sure to be attended with more or less clashing and discord. But whatever compacting and unifying of peoples and sections of the earth is seemingly brought about by the agency of war is really not due to it at all, but to the federative elements in men and society which work out their ends in some measure in spite of war and in the very midst of the disasters which it produces. If these federative forces were not present war would always be disintegrating, or if it produced unity at all, it would be the unity of death and of slavery, whose evil effects would have to be repaired before any real social progress could be made. No one ought, therefore, to be blinded as to the real nature of war because of its seemingly beneficent agency in working out, in certain cases, the desired unity of peoples and sections of the earth.

An international state presupposes international citizenship. At first thought such a thing might seem impracticable. But if one can be a citizen of Pennsylvania and of the United States at the same time, and enjoy the privileges and feel the sacred obligations of both, why might he not just as easily be a citizen of a world state and of some particular nation simultaneously? The elements of an international citizenship already exist. People of different nations not only travel everywhere, but stop and live, own property and do business, pay taxes and submit to authority, among all other peoples. They retain the rights of citizens at home, and expect and receive most of the rights of citizenship among other peoples. Considerable numbers of these, though not expatriating themselves, never return to the country of their formal citizenship. The principle is now recog-

nized practically everywhere that a man
has the right to live anywhere he wishes
on the surface of the planet, to keep his
local citizenship where he wants it, and
at the same time to enjoy all the rights,
privileges and immunities of local citizenship where he resides, except governmental
rights in constitutional countries. All this
development of international rights and
privileges in our day points to a time not
very far in the future when men shall literally be citizens of the world, and a world
government suitable to the needs of world
citizenship shall be set up for them.

Along with this international citizenship,
the beginnings of an international or world
government already exist, — legislative, executive, judicial, — in a decidedly chaotic
state, it is true, but with signs of coming
order. During this century international
congresses have several times met to deter-
mine certain questions of common interest,
as the Congress of Vienna at the close of
the Napoleonic campaigns, the Congress of

Paris after the Crimean war, the Congress of Berlin at the close of the Russo-Turkish conflict, and the Congress of Brussels to regulate certain interests in Africa. The Brussels Congress was a great development in humanity over that of Vienna, and even over the two intervening ones. Why should not such a congress, as Professor John Fiske has recently suggested,[1] meet frequently in the future, ultimately become a congress of all nations, and finally meet at stated times — say once in ten or twenty years — and in a fixed place or places? There is nothing irrational or impossible in the supposition, and the trend of affairs is certainly in that direction.

The idea of a congress of nations was a favorite one with the early advocates of peace, and was thoroughly elaborated by them.[2] Along with it went the idea of a high court of nations. Such a court is

[1] See Mr. Fiske's article on " The Arbitration Treaty " in *The Atlantic Monthly* for February, 1897.

[2] *Essay on a Congress of Nations*, by William Ladd.

likely to be evolved out of the arbitration tribunals and temporary international commissions now so frequently constituted for the settlement of various questions raised in the course of present international intercourse. A high court of nations may become a fixed institution even before a congress of nations comes to meet regularly. The judiciary is becoming more and more influential in our time, and is destined, perhaps, to lead the way in the creation of the great international organization of which I am speaking. The various congresses and conferences which are now annually held to promote the cause of universal peace are laying particular emphasis upon the idea of a permanent international tribunal of arbitration to take the place of the temporary tribunals constituted for the adjustment of differences as they arise. As yet, however, no governments have officially taken action in harmony with advanced public thought on this subject, and it can only be matter of conjecture whether a court of nations will precede a congress, or a congress a court, or whether both will come into existence simultaneously.

Among the beginnings of an international government may also be mentioned the generally recognized principles of international law,[1] the treaties of commerce now so numerous and important, the postal and telegraph unions in which many nations participate, and the modern diplomatic and consular service which binds all nations together in real political bonds. It is an actual fact of present international politics that every nation — every civilized nation at any rate — assists in governing, and is in turn partially governed by, every other nation, either directly through resident diplomacy, or indirectly through the power of collective public opinion expressing itself in

[1] See J. K. Bluntschli's *Die Bedeutung und die Fortschritte des modernen Völkerrechts.* See, also, the recent work of Professor T. J. Lawrence, *The Principles of International Law.* All the recent works on international law give more or less attention to the subject of peace and the means of maintaining it.

the rules of international law or in various forms of concerted international activity for what is supposed to be the common good. There is much that is crude and selfish, and not a little that is inhuman and cruel, in this incipient international government as we now see it evolving; but there is also something that is in the truest sense humane and Christian, and this latter is clearly increasing with the passing of each decade. The public opinion of the world society, as it is now capable of expressing itself with such swiftness and concentration, is sure to force the cruel and the unjust more and more into the background and to establish the good and the helpful.

At first thought, the management of a world government might seem to be attended with insuperable difficulties, because of the extent of territory over which its administration would extend and the great variety of national character and institutions with which it might supposedly have to deal. But really, with our present means of rapid travel and practically instantaneous communication by telegraph and cable, the management of such a government from a single centre would be much easier than it was fifty years ago to govern Ohio from Washington, or the north of England from London. Its administration would also be comparatively easy because its jurisdiction would be limited to a few great subjects of universal character, all purely national affairs being managed as now by the respective nations in the exercise of their local sovereignty. It is no more difficult to administer the government of the United States than it is that of the State of Pennsylvania or of Ohio, and less so than it is that of a great complex, compact municipality like the city of New York or Chicago. The farther removed government is from the entanglements and friction of conflicting local interests and the more it deals only with matters of wide general interest, the easier its administration becomes. For these reasons it does not seem irrational to suppose that a world government might prove in practice the easiest of all governments to administer, at least from the point of view of these objections.

As to the enforcement of the legal enactments of the world government, little difficulty might be expected. An international police is certainly not impossible, if it should ever be needed to enforce the decrees of a congress of nations. Such a state as we are supposing will not, however, be established until arbitration generally prevails and war is practically a thing of the past. Law will then need few, if any, sanctions, and force will play a very small part in its execution. The sense of honor and loyalty to right will prove amply sufficient to secure obedience. The chief functions of the government of the world state will be legislative and judicial, and its executive duties will be .largely those of simple direction and guidance rather than of compulsion.

With the setting up of this world state,

whose establishment is demanded by the as yet unfulfilled destiny of the race and clearly indicated by the progress of society, the peace of the world, so far as that means the cessation of war, will be forever sealed. International chaos and anarchy, as they now so deplorably exist, will have passed away. Many of the vexatious questions with which national governments now have to deal, arising as they do from international complications, will disappear. National governments, like our present state governments, will then make it their business to care for and promote the national interests — the real interests of the people — and not to meddle with the affairs of other peoples, which is now considered in some countries the chief mark of statesmanship. The general effect of all this in the further promotion of industrial and social prosperity and peace, of education and religion, will be magical. The whole of human society will feel at all points a thrill of new life and hope. Reason, conscience and law will be enthroned. Love and goodwill will then be considered strong and worthy motives, as is none too frequently the case now.

Such an organization will not mean the stagnation or the end of civilization. On the contrary, it is the presupposition of a civilization which shall be truly human and Christian, and hence vigorous and strong. The thought, the energy, the material wealth, now consumed in destructive rivalry will be turned into beneficent coöperative enterprises, and the earth will for the first time in its history really begin to "blossom like the garden of the Lord." Above all, the spirits of men, delivered from the bondage of hate and fear, from which but few anywhere under present conditions wholly escape, will be free to enter into each other's thoughts, purposes and attainments, in a spontaneous, natural way, which will make of the whole race a wise, strong, prosperous and happy brotherhood, such as we have so far seen in but small por-

tions of it. The end of the reign of international hate, — the beginning of the reign
of universal brotherhood, — who can measure either its spiritual or its material significance ?

I do not delude myself into supposing
that such a state of states as that here indicated can be artificially created, as the
French philosophers would have constructed
off-hand their social compact.[1] States grow
before they are\ made. Their formal constitution, if they are to be anything more
than temporary structures, is the last act
in a drama extending over long periods. So
will it be with the federation of the world
in an international state. What leads me
to believe that such a federation is comparatively near is that the forces and processes which are evolving it have been long
working, and that in recent years the products of their working — swift, uniform and
well-nigh universal — have become so man-

---

[1] *Du contrat social, ou principes du droit politique*, by
J. J. Rousseau.

ifest and so numerous that the significance
of it all cannot be mistaken. When the
wheat is knee-high in the field one is justi-
fied in believing that the harvest time will
come soon, unless the course of nature goes
awry. The great idea of a world federation
in some form has gotten clearly into men's
minds. It is too powerful, too attractive
and inspiring, to be resisted. It appeals,
both on the material and the spiritual side,
to the deepest needs and to the loftiest
hopes of the race. All obstacles to its
realization will be broken down, if not to-
morrow, then afterwards. How soon, will
depend largely on the purpose, the intelligence, the heart, which those already possessed of the great idea shall put into the
work of reconstructing and reorganizing
humanity on a world basis. War, with its
desolations and incredible follies, may still
sweep over portions of the earth while the
demons of distrust and violence are being
cast out. But its days are nearly numbered.
Its glory is fast turning to shame. It is

everywhere on the defensive. The great federative movement, which has been gathering strength for nearly twice a thousand years of Christian progress, — nay, in whose pulses is beating the growing life of all the human ages, — will peacefully occupy the places of ruins left of war, and will build at last a temple and city of concord for the whole earth, within whose holy gates the noise of battle shall never be heard.

Tennyson's dream will then be more than realized ; there will be no longer any battle-flags to furl.

APPENDIX

The Czar's Rescript calling for a Conference on Reduction of Armaments

ISSUED AT ST. PETERSBURG BY COUNT MURAVIEFF ON
THE 24TH OF AUGUST, 1898

THE maintenance of general peace and the possible reduction of the excessive armaments which weigh upon all nations present themselves in existing conditions to the whole world as an ideal toward which the endeavors of all governments should be directed. The humanitarian and magnanimous ideas of His Majesty the Emperor, my august master, have been won over to this view in the conviction that this lofty aim is in conformity with the most essential interests and legitimate views of all the powers ; and the imperial government thinks the present moment would be very favorable to seeking the means.

International discussion is the most effectual means of insuring all peoples' benefit, — a real durable peace, above all, — putting an end to the progressive development of the present armaments.

In the course of the last twenty years the longing for general appeasement has grown especially pronounced in the consciences of civilized nations, and the preservation of peace has been put forward as an object of international policy. It is in its name that great states have concluded, among themselves, powerful alliances.

It is the better to guarantee peace that they have developed, in proportions hitherto unprecedented, their military forces and still continue to increase them, without shrinking from any sacrifice. Nevertheless, all these efforts have not yet been able to bring about the beneficent result desired, pacification.

The financial charges, following the upward march, strike at the very root of public prosperity. The intellectual and physical strength of the nations' labor and capital are mostly diverted from their natural application and are unproductively consumed. Hundreds of millions are devoted to acquiring terrible engines of destruction, which, though to-day regarded as the last work of science, are destined to-morrow to lose all their value in consequence of some fresh discovery in the same field.

National culture, economic progress and the production of wealth are either paralyzed or checked in development. Moreover, in proportion as the armaments of each power increase, they less and less fulfill the object the governments have set before themselves. The economic crisis, due in great part to the system of armaments *à outrance*, and the continual danger which lies in this massing of war material are transforming the armed peace of our days into a crushing burden which the peoples have more and more difficulty in bearing.

It appears evident that if this state of things were to be prolonged, it would inevitably lead to the very cataclysm it is desired to avert, and the horrors whereof make every thinking being shudder in advance. To put an end to these incessant armaments, and to seek the means of warding off the calamities which are threatening the whole world, is the supreme duty to-day imposed upon all states.

Filled with this idea, His Majesty has been pleased to command me to propose to all the governments whose representatives you are, accredited to the imperial court, the assembling of a conference which shall occupy itself with this grave problem.

This conference will be, by the help of God, a happy presage for the century which is about to open. It would converge into one powerful focus the efforts of all states sincerely seeking to make the great conception of universal peace triumph over the elements of trouble and discord, and it would, at the same time, cement their agreement by a corporate consecration of the principles of equity and right whereon rest the security of states and the welfare of peoples.